DESIGN · GRAPHICS

·drawing and presenting your design ideas ·

· david fair · marilyn kenny ·

HODDER AND STOUGHTON
LONDON SYDNEY AUCKLAND TORONTO

Preface

Design Graphics provides a practical pupil's guide to visual communication and design drawing skills. It is of particular relevance to students involved in all Craft, Design and Technology courses, from the early years onwards, to examination level. In this book, graphic communication is approached as an integral part of the design process in which drawing and the presentation of ideas are recognised as important design tools.

Design Graphics offers a structured course of study, whilst at the same time meets the need for a handy reference manual of design presentation techniques. There is a progression from the simplest elements needed to record ideas, to more elaborate techniques which may be used to communicate final designs. The material is presented in broad sections rather than chapters, and each page within the sections is self-contained and titled. Although each page can be referred to individually, the pages are interrelated, and allow for easy cross-referencing.

The text is fully supported by design based assignments, which provide the opportunity to practise the techniques shown in the book.

Acknowledgements

The Authors would like to thank the following for their help in providing material for the preparation of this book: Mick Beech, J.C. Lampson, C. Ruddell — Styling Department, Jaguar Cars Ltd, Coventry, J. Stanley — Sheffield City Polytechnic, Students of the Industrial Design Department, Lanchester Polytechnic, J.D. Hughes, T. Paplauskas, A.V.M. Kitchens and Bedrooms, Rugby, The Design Council, The Boilerhouse, Victoria and Albert Museum, Lego U.K. Ltd, Rotring U.K., British Standards Institute and Her Majesty The Queen (through the Royal Library, Windsor Castle) for the da Vinci on page 5. Book and cover-design are by David Fair.

Special thanks are due to Sue Sanders for typing the text, and to Julie Fair for her support and patience during the preparation of this book.

Series editor David Shaw

British Library Cataloguing in Publication Data

Fair, David
    Design graphics.
    1. Communication in design.
    I. Title II. Insert Kenny Marilyn
    745.4   NK1510

ISBN 0 340 40529 5

First published 1987
Sixth impression 1990

Typeset by Graphicraft, Hong Kong for Hodder and Stoughton Educational a division of Hodder and Stoughton Ltd. Mill Road Dunton Green. Sevenoaks, Kent and printed in Hong Kong by Colorcraft Ltd.

Contents

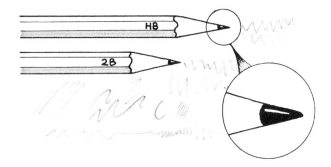

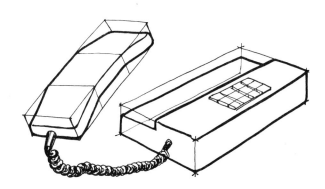

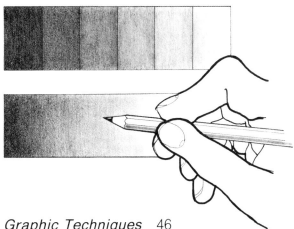

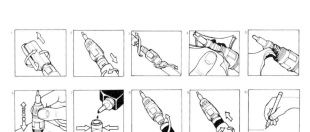

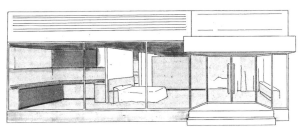

The Language of Design

When you are solving a design problem, it is useful to put your ideas down on paper at an early stage. Notes or sketches will enable you to picture these ideas in your mind and help you to make decisions about them. It is easier to choose the best solution from a series of sketches drawn on paper, than it is to try to compare them all in your head. Drawing is also a very good way of recording these ideas which otherwise might easily be forgotten. Your drawings will also show other people exactly what you are thinking.

It is far easier to show someone a picture than to rely entirely on words. You could prove this yourself by describing your route home from school in two ways:

(i) make a written description of your journey, and

(ii) draw a simple map or plan of the route. The drawing should make it easier for you to explain the route. It should also be easier for others to understand.

In the written description you have used the language of words to communicate your message to another person. In the drawing you have used visual communication — the language of pictures.

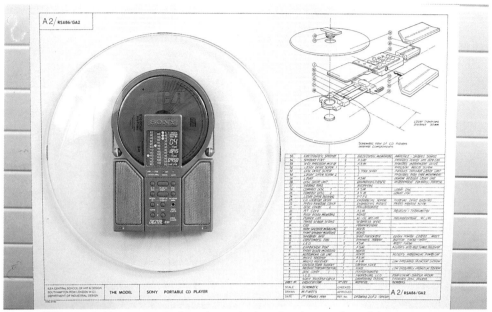

Martin Witts: portable compact disc player design drawing and model

In all areas of design, people use drawing to help them solve problems and to record their thoughts.

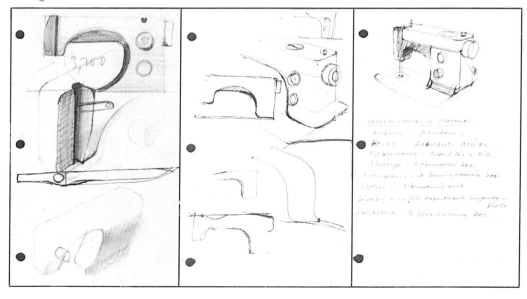

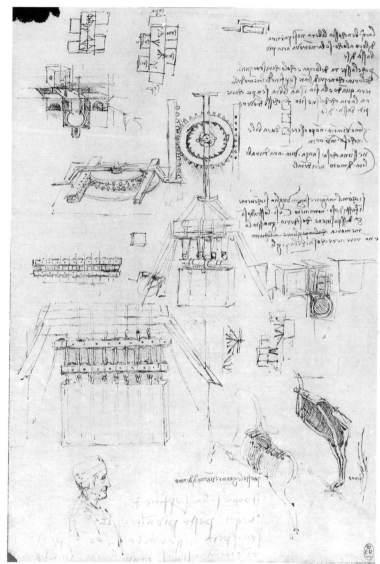

Leonardo da Vinci: studies for the casting of a bronze horse

Ken Grange; pages from his sketchbook

The Line Up . . .

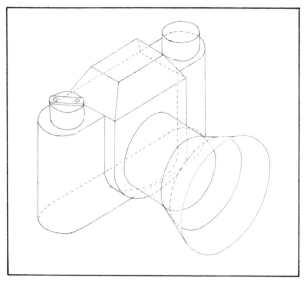

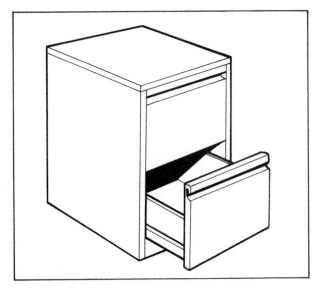

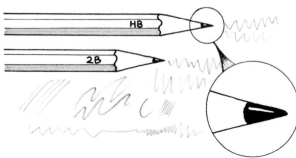

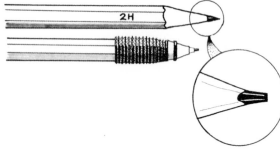

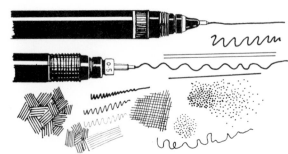

Soft pencil

Pencils are graded according to their hardness or softness. These grades range from 6B (very soft) to 9H (very hard). A soft pencil will give a blacker line and lose its point more quickly than a hard pencil. Even with only one pencil, the lines that you can make will vary according to how you use your pencil. You can press harder or draw the pencil over the paper quickly to produce different types of line. An HB pencil can be used for most types of drawing. Softer pencils do not need as much pressure to make a line and this makes them ideal for quick design sketches.

Hard pencil

Pencils which range from grades H to 9H are harder than the B grades. This means that they keep their point for a longer time, and do not need to be sharpened as often. Therefore the line thickness is more even, which makes these pencils the most useful for accurate drawings, especially those where precise measurements are involved.

For greatest accuracy the points of these pencils must be sharpened to a needle-like point or a chisel-like edge.

Technical pens

Technical pens produce lines of a constant thickness, and so are useful for drawings that need to be accurate. They also produce bold, clear lines which can be photocopied, or printed with good results. Unlike most other pens or pencils, technical pens should be held at about 90° to the surface of the paper i.e. upright. It is important to replace the cap of the pen when not in use, so that the ink does not dry in the nib and the drawing tip is protected. (Recommended nib sizes for beginners are: 0.35 mm; 0.5 mm; 0.7 mm.)

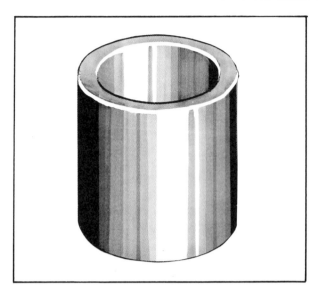

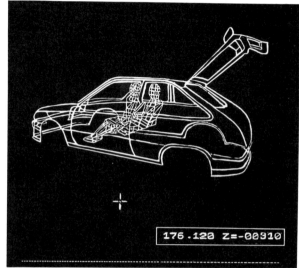

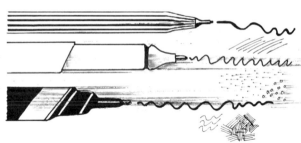

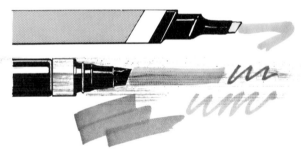

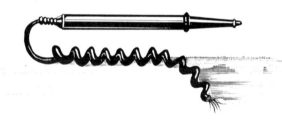

Fine-line markers

These markers have fine or extra fine tips and are produced in a few basic colours. Fine-line markers are popular because they can be used like pencils for quick design sketches, yet also give a thin bold line similar to a technical pen. They can be used to line-in more precise drawings, cross-hatch sectional views (page 49), or apply texture to a drawing. (pages 36 and 41). Fine-line markers are also useful for notemaking and lettering.

Studio markers

Studio markers are widely used by designers as one of the basic tools for design drawing. They offer a fast method of adding colour and interest to more developed drawings. When used more carefully they can be effective in producing very finished presentation drawings — drawings which give a clearer picture of what a finished design may actually look like.

Computer-aided drawing

Many designers now use a computer to produce drawings which are shown on visual display units (VDUs). This type of drawing is likely to be produced using a keyboard rather than a pen or pencil, but on some computers a light-pen is used to 'draw' on the screen of the VDU. Although using a computer does not always save time when making the original drawing, it does allow the designer to change or copy the drawings quickly. They can also be stored in the computer's memory for future reference. (See page 62.)

Line of action

Figure 8

Drawing your designs will trigger off new and different ideas. To help this flow of thinking, it is important to be able to put your thoughts on paper quickly. How can we do this? Look at the picture of the skier (figure 8:1). Can you draw this figure using only *six* lines? Think of the lines that you use as a framework.

This simple type of line drawing is enough to show the structure of the figure (figure 8:2). The little metal skier in the picture (figure 8:3) was based on a line drawing. The lines have been copied in wire and brazed together. The angle or curve of lines can give the idea of movement. The pictures above show figures in action (figures. 8:4–8:7). Try to capture the action of these figures using a few quick lines.

By varying the pressure on a pencil it is possible to produce lines which are bold or faint. Faint lines are useful in planning a drawing as *guidelines* when drawing more complex shapes. These lines should not be too dark as they are not the most important feature of the drawing.

In drawing a shape which is to be symmetrical (one which is identical on both sides of a centre line) a faint centre line is very useful. The centre line is called the axis of symmetry and can be drawn in lightly with a pencil.

Look at the examples on this page. You will see that all the designs are drawn over a structure of guidelines. These guidelines help to plot out proportions and keep drawings on a straight line.

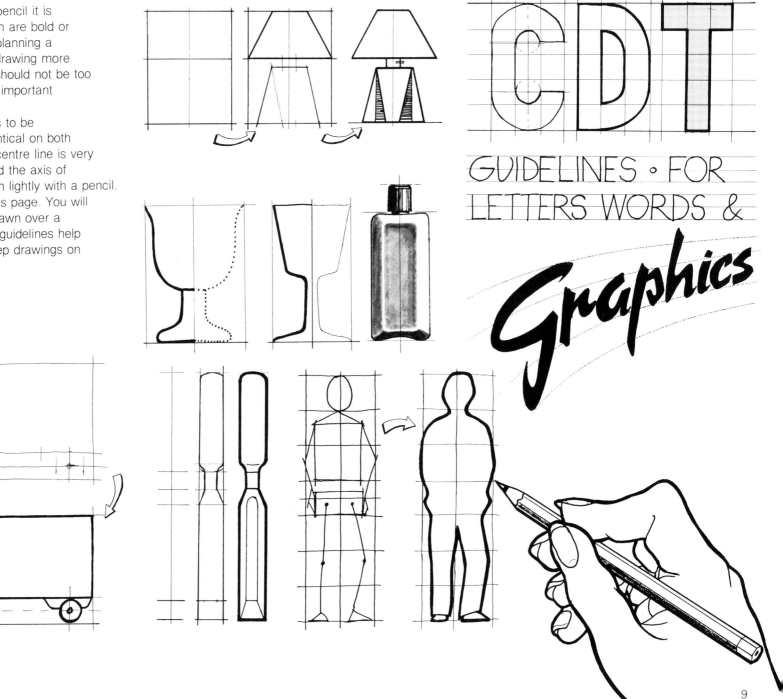

CDT

GUIDELINES · FOR LETTERS WORDS & Graphics

Lines Around Us

The pictures show some examples of lines in our surroundings. Lines on living things can serve to attract, to disguise, or to act as a warning to enemies. The wide black lines on zebras break up the outline of the animal and make it difficult to see against its surroundings. This is known as camouflage, which helps to protect the animal. Can you think of any other examples of camouflage using lines?

The stripes on the snake are very noticeable. These act as a warning — *stay away*! However, the spider's web is made up of thin, delicate lines that form an intricate structure to trap insects. The effects of lines have been used by Man for similar reasons. For example, the rugby shirt has wide horizontal bands that make the wearer appear broader than he really is. Obviously he now seems a larger and more frightening opponent.

Bold lines have been used on the traffic signs in the picture. They are intended to stand out and provide instant warnings for motorists.

Once you become aware of lines in your surroundings, you may be surprised to see just how often they occur. You will see them on notices, signs, furniture, clothing and packaging. Look at the structures and buildings around you. Even on cars and down the middle of the road, you will see lines.

Try making a list of as many lines as you can see in just five minutes. Can you work out the purpose of the lines? Are they acting as warnings or decoration, or do they serve some other purpose?

Line as Decoration

Designers often use lines to decorate surfaces. The interesting use of different types of line can make a dull object look very attractive (figure 11:1). Lines can emphasise a particular feature and help make an impact. For example, wallpaper with strong vertical lines will tend to make a room appear high and narrow. Lines can even be used to create optical illusions (figure 11:2). Can you see why this is an illusion?

Certain patterns of lines trigger off feelings and emotions in people. Designers use this knowledge to create a particular mood or effect. You can see this yourself by looking at the window blinds in figures 11:3 and 11:4.

Figure 11:3 has gently curving and graceful lines which produce a feeling of calm. Figure 11:4 is decorated with jagged, angular lines that are sharp, suggesting a feeling of tension and energy. Which do you think is the more suitable design for a bedroom?

Figure 11

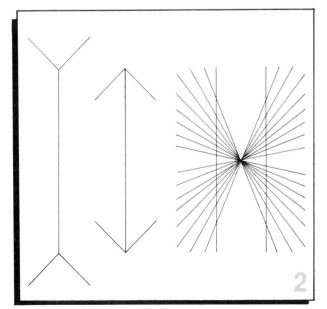

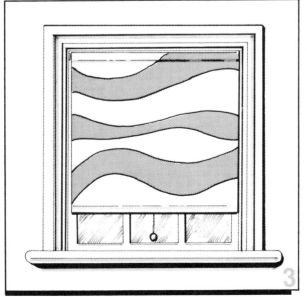

Shaping Up

Have you noticed that as you draw lines you create shapes? Shapes emerge when lines enclose spaces. The lines around the shapes are the outlines. The simplest way to describe an object is to draw its shape using an outline.

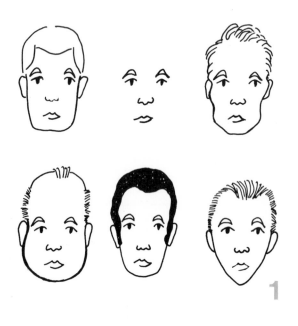

Figure 12

Look at the heads drawn above (figure 12:1). Can you see how a very slight change in the curve or angle of a line can completely alter the shape and character of the face? For this reason it is very important to use lines carefully in order to make your drawings clear.

You can explore a design idea by making slight alterations to a shape and changing its outline (figure 12:2).

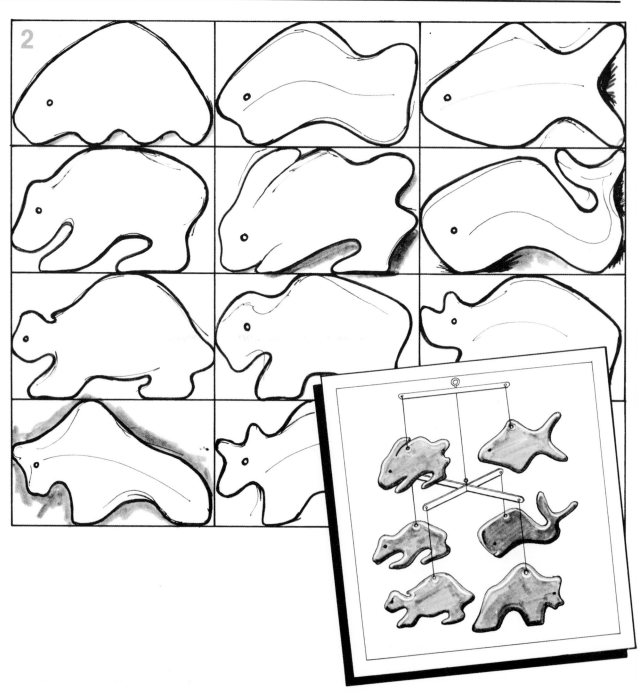

Designing with Shapes 1

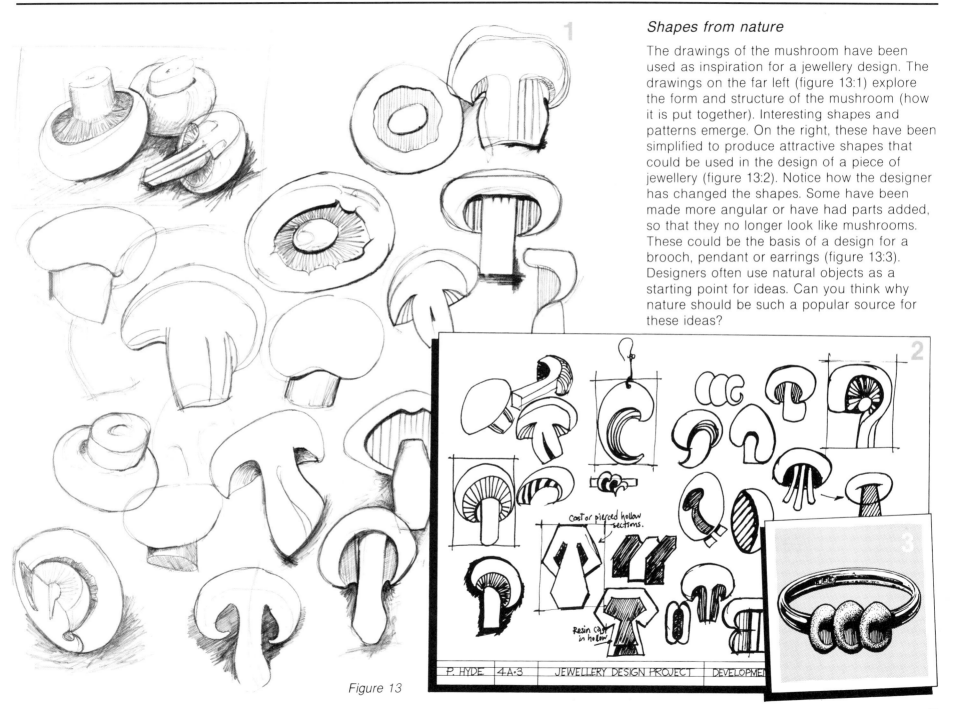

Shapes from nature

The drawings of the mushroom have been used as inspiration for a jewellery design. The drawings on the far left (figure 13:1) explore the form and structure of the mushroom (how it is put together). Interesting shapes and patterns emerge. On the right, these have been simplified to produce attractive shapes that could be used in the design of a piece of jewellery (figure 13:2). Notice how the designer has changed the shapes. Some have been made more angular or have had parts added, so that they no longer look like mushrooms. These could be the basis of a design for a brooch, pendant or earrings (figure 13:3). Designers often use natural objects as a starting point for ideas. Can you think why nature should be such a popular source for these ideas?

Figure 13

Cast or pierced hollow sections.

Resin cast in hollow

P. HYDE   4A·3   JEWELLERY DESIGN PROJECT   DEVELOPMEN

Designing with Shapes 2

Geometrical shapes

The drawings on this page show how geometric shapes — circles, hexagons, triangles etc. — can be used at the start of a design idea. How many examples of these types of shapes can you find in the room? You will notice that these shapes are not only used as decoration or pattern, but they often form the basic structure of an object. For example, look at the shapes that make up an electricity pylon or a honey-comb (figure 14.1).

A number of simple geometric shapes can be used as a guide or framework for drawing objects (figures 14:2 and 14:3)

Many organisations and companies use geometric shapes in their trademark or logo (the symbols that identify the company or its products). (See figure 14:4.) What is the advantage of using these simple shapes in a logo?

Geometric grids can be used to develop interesting patterns for decoration. By using a grid, the pattern can be repeated accurately as in wallpaper or fabric design (figure 14:5). These grids are not always based on squares like graph paper, but can be triangular or diamond shaped etc. (figure 14:6).

Figure 14

selected for the
DESIGN
CENTRE
LONDON

CLOCK PROJECT

Developing 3-D Shapes

Many of the shapes we have been looking at on the previous pages, have been 'flat' shapes. They have two measurements or *dimensions* — length and width.

By cutting and folding a flat shape, we can create a *three-dimensional form*. The form has length, width and thickness — three dimensions. Figure 15:1 shows an arrangement of six squares which together could be cut out of card and folded to make a cube. The drawing of an object opened out in this way is called a *development*. A development can be used as a pattern for cutting out objects which are made from materials in sheet form (e.g. plastics, metal or card). They provide us with a guide for cutting and bending. Using a development also means that we can make a fold instead of joining every separated piece.

Carefully open out a cardboard package and study its development. Can you see the way it has been folded? You may also notice the flaps that enable the box to be neatly glued together.

There are other ways of developing a cube. Draw a different method to the one shown on this page. Cut it out and test it. Use it in the design of a package for:
(i) paper tissues, or
(ii) a fragile Christmas decoration.

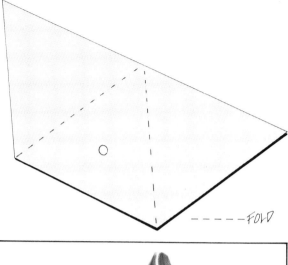

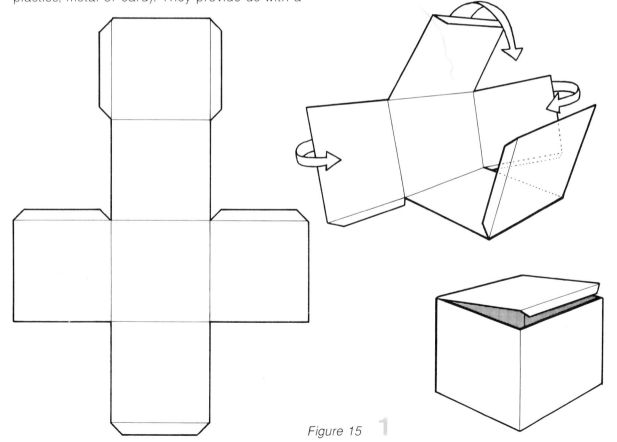

Figure 15 1

Assignments 1

1 Collect some magazine photographs or ask a partner to pose in action positions. Make some very quick line drawings of them and try to capture their pose. Use these drawings to design a small sculpture or balancing figure. (See page 8.)

2 A water storage tank is to be installed in a nature reserve. Design a cover (or paint scheme) for the tank that will help it blend into its surroundings. (See page 10.)

3 Mugs are often used as gift or souvenir items, and have a message or design on them. Prepare designs and developments for a package to contain a souvenir mug. Your package must allow the design on the mug to be be seen (figure 16.1).

4 Design a package for one of the items listed below. Use lines as the main decoration.
(i)   Panel pins/screws
(ii) pencils/crayons
(iii) pots of paint
(See page 11.)

5 A childs playroom is in need of decoration. Using a pattern of lines, design a wallpaper that will make the room seem cheerful and lively. (See page 11.)

6 Select a tool from the workshops such as a hammer or pliers. Look at it carefully and draw it with the aid of guidelines. (See pages 9 and 14.)

7 Logograms are trademarks or symbols used to identify a business or company. They are often simply called logos. Copy three popular logos, drawing the guidelines on which you think they were constructed, for instance circles, squares, triangles, axes of symmetry, etc. (See pages 9 and 14.)

8 Design a pattern for a border of tiles based on a grid. The pattern should repeat itself at least three times and be suitable for use in either:
(i)   a bathroom, or
(ii) a kitchen, or
(iii) a subway.
(See pages 11 and 14.)

9 Use a natural object as the basis of a series of drawings (e.g. a shell or cactus).
(a) Produce a carefully observed drawing of the object.
(b) Draw a section of the object (enlarged to fill the paper).
(c) Draw a stylised or much simplified version. (Use a fine-line marker or ball point pen).
Select some of the interesting shapes that emerge from your drawings and use these as the starting point for designing either:
(i)   a piece of jewellery, or
(ii) a fabric design, or
(iii) a pattern of veneers.
(See page 13.)

Figure 16 1

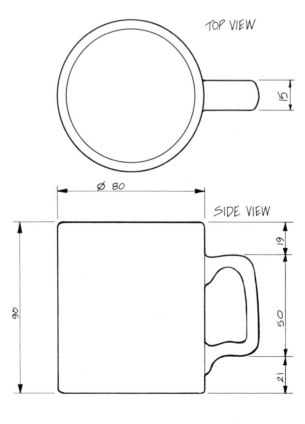

TOP VIEW

Ø 80

SIDE VIEW

Pictorial Drawing

On the right you can see a number of different drawings of a matchbox (figures 17:2–17:7). These different ways of drawing are all types of *pictorial drawing*, and are used when a more realistic impression or picture is needed. What is the difference between these drawings and the drawing of the matchbox below? (Figure 17:1.)

Look carefully and you will see that the most important feature of the drawings on the right is that they show three dimensions. Write down the names of these three dimensions.

Figure 17:1 shows the length and width of the matchbox, but it appears to be flat. By adding a third dimension — the thickness — into the drawings, the other matchboxes all appear to be solid and not flat. This third dimension is what makes a pictorial drawing different from a flat view or elevation.

Each drawing shows a different view of the matchbox, and each can be used to give a particular impression or effect. For example, one of the drawings makes the matchbox look as though it towers over its surroundings. Another drawing gives us the impression of looking down on the matchbox.

In the following pages you will see how you can make drawing like these, and the examples shown will help you to decide which method is best used for a particular purpose.

Figure 17

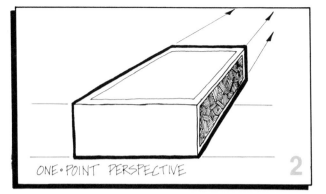

ONE·POINT PERSPECTIVE

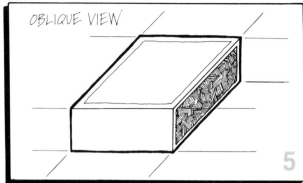

TWO·POINT PERSPECTIVE

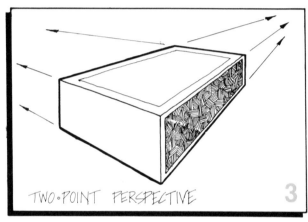

THREE·POINT PERSPECTIVE

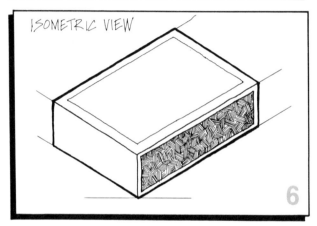

OBLIQUE VIEW

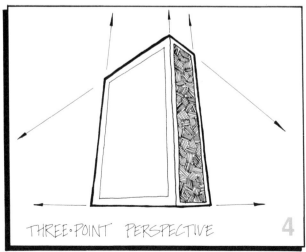

ISOMETRIC VIEW

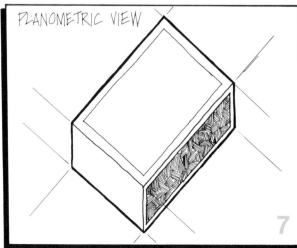

PLANOMETRIC VIEW

Perspective

Have you ever noticed that the further away something is from us, the smaller it appears to be? You may also have noticed how parallel railway lines appear to meet in the distance (figure 18:1).

A *perspective* drawing recreates the illusion of objects getting smaller and parallel lines converging (getting closer together) as they get further away from us. Because perspective drawings are very similar to the way we actually see things, they can be easily understood by most people.

Figure 18

Perspective first began to be understood when artists looked at objects through screens or windows (figure 18:2). They noticed that if they drew around the shapes of the object onto the glass in front of them, the result would be a realistic looking picture. In fact, the word 'perspective' comes from a Latin word, 'perspecta' which means to look through.

You could try this idea out for yourself (figure 18:3). Look straight in front of you through a window or sheet of clear acrylic, cover or close one eye, and draw around the outline of an object onto the glass or acrylic with a wax pencil. You will find that you have transferred the *three-dimensions* of the object to a *two-dimensional* surface (the glass or acrylic). This surface is referred to as the *picture plane*. When we draw the perspective view onto paper, we are imagining the paper in place of the glass window.

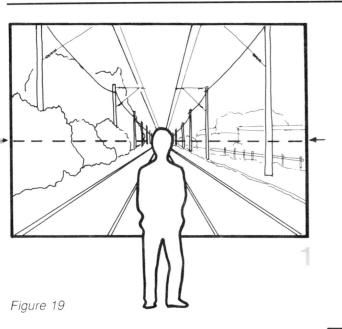

HORIZON LINE

V.P. 1   V.P. 2

Figure 19

Vanishing points and horizon lines

In figure 19:1 the railway line shown on page 18, has been simplified into a drawing using a few lines. The tracks appear to meet at a point in the distance. This is known as the *vanishing point*. Notice that the vanishing point is situated on a horizontal line — *the horizon line* — which runs across the picture. This line matches the height of the viewer's eyes, and is sometimes called the *eye level*.

Figure 19:2 shows a photograph of a multi-storey building. You can clearly see that the sides of the building appear to get smaller as they recede (get further away). In this picture there are two vanishing points where each set of lines converge and meet, to the left and right of the building. Notice that the horizon line is not easy to see, as there are other buildings or objects restricting our view. However, we can find the position of the horizon or eye level by joining together the two vanishing points.

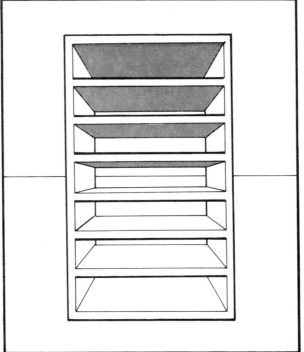

The vanishing points and horizon are the most important features in any perspective drawing, and their position will decide how the final drawing will look. It is important to decide what you wish to show before you begin your drawing. Which side of the object do you wish to see? Will it be above your eye level or below? (See figures 19:3 and 19:4.)

Low horizon - low eye level   *High horizon - high eye level*

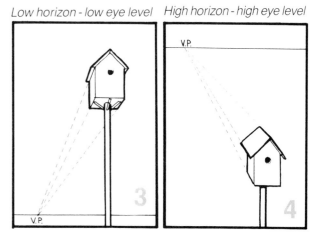

One-Point Perspective 1

One-point perspective is the simplest type of perspective to draw because it is based on a 'flat' view of an object. Depth lines are drawn only to one vanishing point. The simplest form of one-point perspective can be drawn without a horizon line.

For example, in figure 20:1 a block letter has been drawn, then faint lines have been drawn from each corner to the vanishing point. The position of the point depends whether you are situated to the left or right, above or below the letter. What position are we in when viewing the letter F in figure 20:1?

The letter has been completed by drawing in the back edges. These are parallel to the front edges. Because the object is in perspective, you cannot measure the depth lines — they must be estimated.

If you place the vanishing point too far to one side of the object you are drawing, it will begin to look distorted (out of shape). Avoid this by positioning it close to the centre of vision, that is, a point close to the centre of the picture (figure 20:2).

An advantage of one-point perspective is that complicated or curved shapes can be drawn as simple flat views and then the depth lines can be projected (drawn) back to the single vanishing point (figure 20:3).

Try drawing one of the letters in the example, but position the vanishing point so that we can see the underside and left-hand side of the letter.

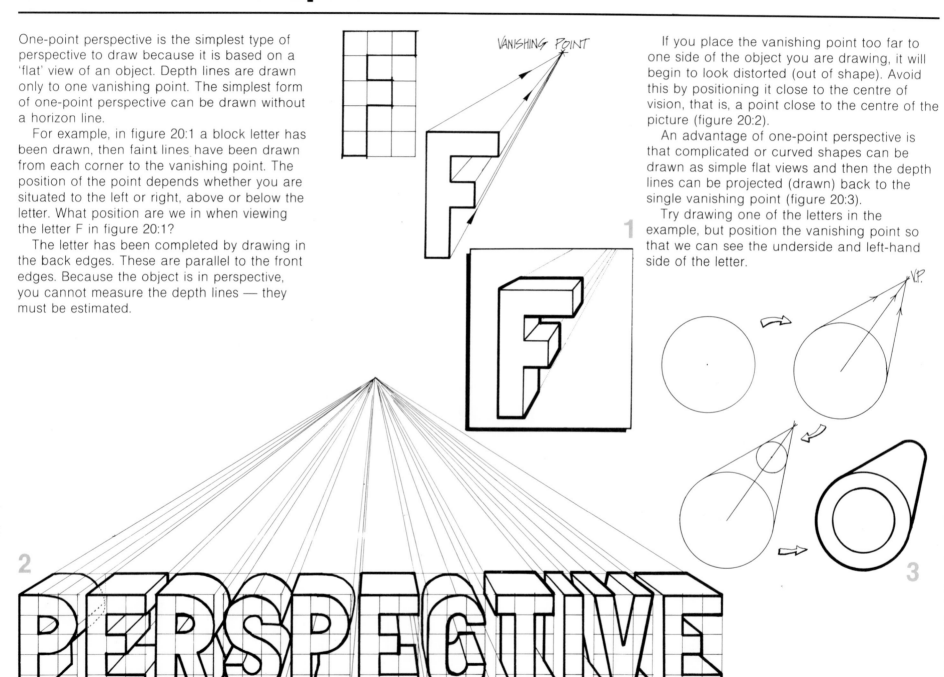

Figure 20

Figure 21

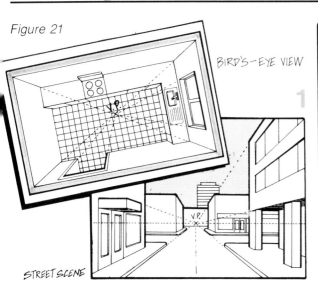

BIRD'S-EYE VIEW

STREET SCENE

In a one-point perspective drawing, the depth lines are projected to only one vanishing point. This type of pictorial drawing is very useful when showing street scenes, 'bird's-eye' views, or rooms viewed directly from the front (figure 21:1).

The following method of drawing an estimated one-point perspective can be used for any of these types of view.

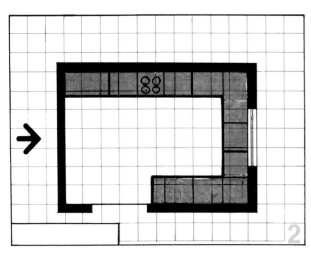

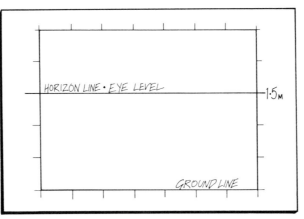

HORIZON LINE · EYE LEVEL — 1.5 M

GROUND LINE

■ Draw a rectangle on the paper and mark off a suitable scale. In this drawing, the rectangle has been drawn to the same proportions as the room shown in the plan (figure 21:2). Draw in the horizon line (eye level) at the required height. A normal eye level will be about 1.5 m above ground-level.

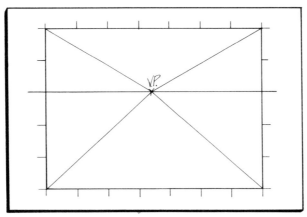

V.P.

■ A vanishing point is now marked on the horizon line. For a *true* one-point perspective view, the point should be exactly half way along the horizon line (centre of vision). Draw in diagonal lines from each corner of the frame to the point.

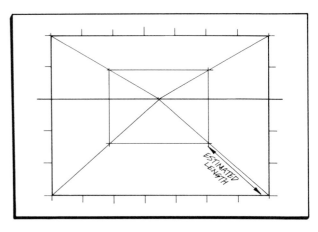

ESTIMATED LENGTH

■ Estimate the depth of the room and draw in the back wall. The diagonal lines should go through each corner.

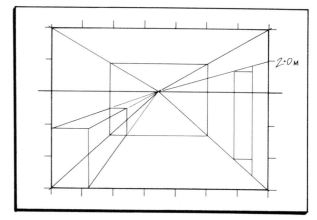

2.0 M

■ Draw in details to the correct height by using the scale marked on the picture frame. For example, to find the height of the door on the side wall, measure 2 m on the scale, and draw a line from that point back to the vanishing point. The width of the door will have to be estimated.
■ Follow this method for drawing in other features in the kitchen. (See page 22.)

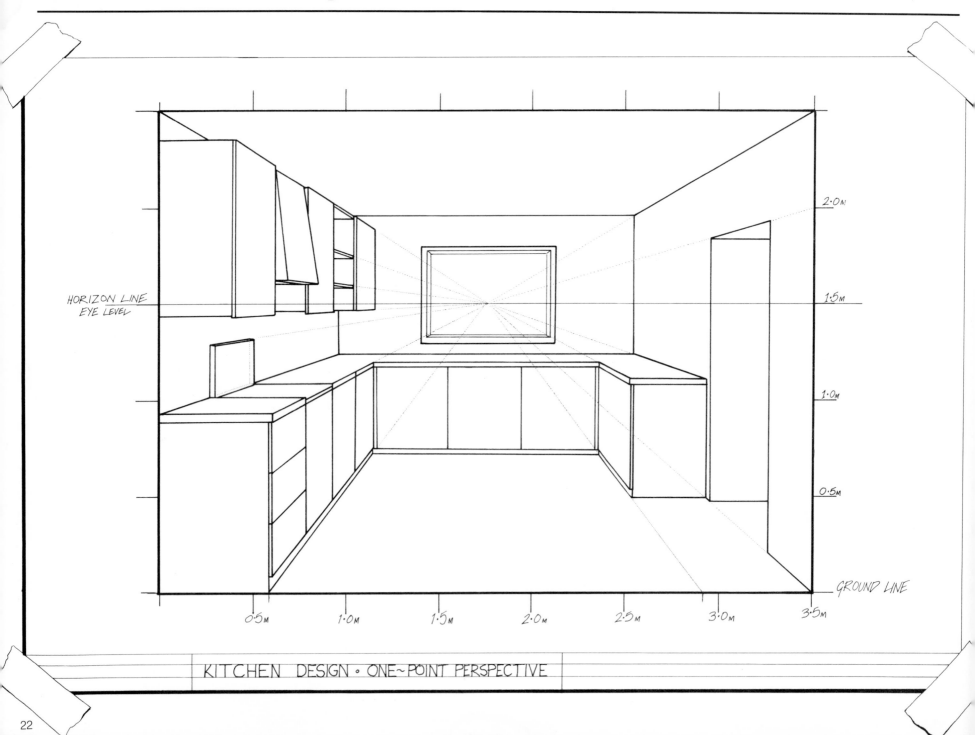

HORIZON LINE
EYE LEVEL

2·0м

1·5м

1·0м

0·5м

GROUND LINE

0·5м   1·0м   1·5м   2·0м   2·5м   3·0м   3·5м

KITCHEN DESIGN · ONE~POINT PERSPECTIVE

You have seen how one-point perspective is a useful method of drawing an object when it is square-on to the viewer (figure 23:1). When the object is placed at an angle however, a corner will be the closest point to the viewer (figure 23:2). Can you see how the sides recede from us in two directions? In order to draw this view, two vanishing points are needed. This is called two-point perspective.

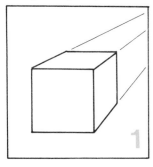
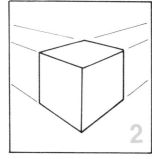

The following text describes a method of drawing two-point perspective by estimation.

- Mark two vanishing points on a horizon line (eye level). These points should not be too close together, as the final drawing will look distorted. In fact they can even be positioned off the paper (figure 23:3).
- Show the nearest edge of the object by drawing a vertical line. This line should be drawn below the horizon line if we are looking down on the object (also figure 23:3).
- Draw faint lines from the top and bottom of the vertical line to each vanishing point (figure 23:4).
- Estimate the length of each side and draw in vertical lines to form the outer edges (figure 23:5).
- Join the tops of the outer edges to the vanishing point furthest from them. Where the lines cross, the back corner of the box is formed (figure 23:6).
- The outline can now be drawn in firmly.

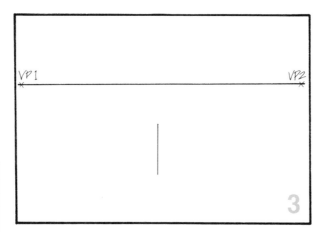

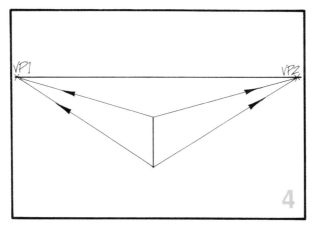

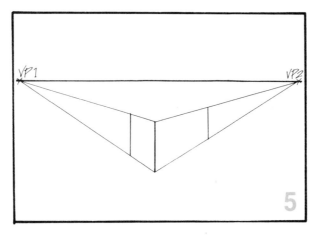

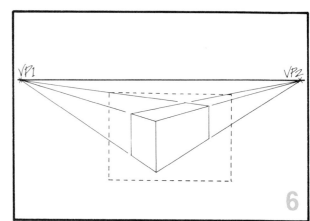

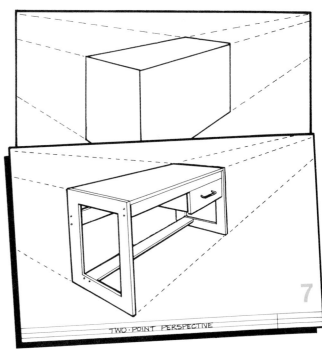

Figure 23

Remember, the object is the important feature on your page, not the space around it. To help the object stand out, frame it with a border or cut out and mount it (figure 23:7).

Two-Point Perspective 2

We can give a different view of an object on any perspective drawing, by placing it above or below the horizon line, or by moving it further to the left or right. In figure 24:1 all the blocks are drawn to the same vanishing points. Can you see that the blocks drawn below the horizon line give us a view of their top surface, while the underside is visible on those placed above the horizon line?

With practice, it is possible to draw without plotting vanishing points and horizon line. In figure 24:2 the lines on the object are directed to imaginary, distant vanishing points. When the vanishing points are close together on a drawing, the object looks very small and distorted (figure 24:3). Distant vanishing points allow us to make larger drawings. This may even include vanishing points which occur off the paper (figure 24:4).

Figure 24

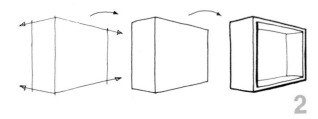

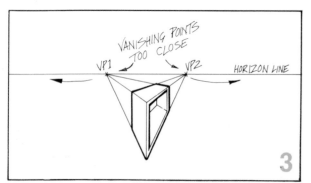

Of all the different methods of pictorial drawing the *oblique view* is probably the most simple. In fact, you may already have drawn something using this system but did not realise it!

In the picture of the matchbox below (figure 25:1) we can look at the front view but learn nothing about the depth of the matchbox. In other words it is *two-dimensional*. (See also page 17.) When drawing an oblique view we can start by using this flat, two-dimensional view (see figure 25:2). The next step is to draw a sloping line at an angle of 45° from the corners of the shape (figure 25:3). These parallel lines will represent the depth of the object being drawn. If you wished to, you could take the measurements of a matchbox and use them to make an accurate, scaled oblique drawing.

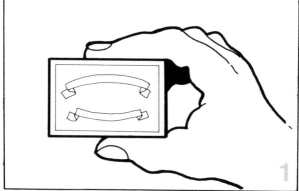

However this would reveal one of the disadvantages of this system. Although the front view of the box can be drawn to scale, the depth lines must be scaled down (usually by half) to stop the object looking distorted. Why do you think it appears distorted if the depth lines are not scaled down?

The effect can be clearly seen when a cube is drawn without scaling the depth lines (figure 25:6).

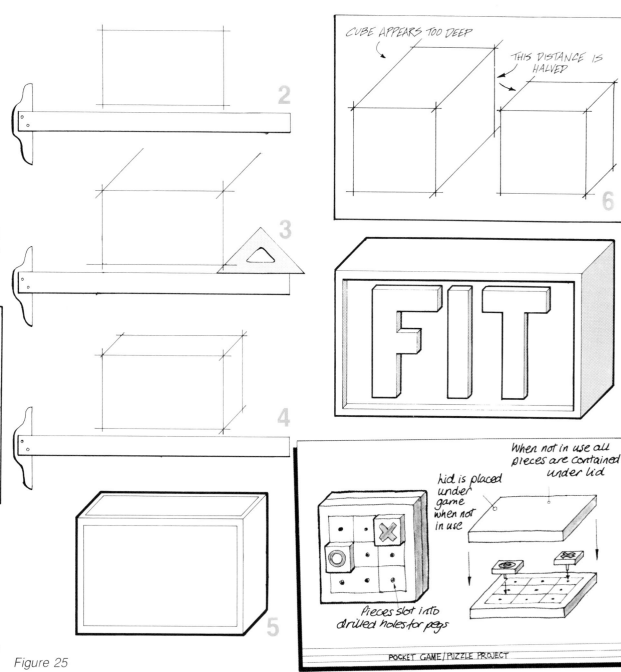

Figure 25

The Oblique View 2

The oblique view is based on a flat view, and so is ideal for drawing objects which have curved or circular surfaces (figure 26:1). It can also be useful when drawing a pictorial view of a more complex shape (figure 26:2). When drawing a shape like this, it is best to begin by drawing the most difficult shape as a flat view constructed inside a frame.

Figure 26

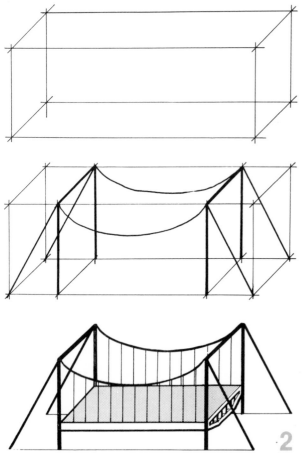

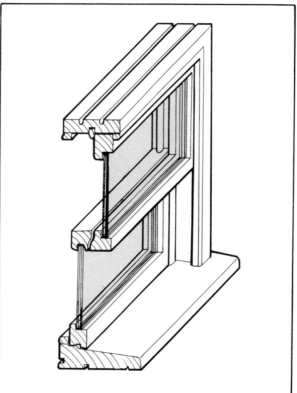

Drawing a cylinder (figure 26:3)

■ Start by drawing the circular end of the cylinder. As this is a flat view and will appear as a true circle, it can be drawn with a compass.

■ Draw a line at 45° from the centre of the circle. Mark off the depth of the shape along the line (remember that this distance is halved, so that the shape does not appear distorted).

■ Draw a second circle — the back of the cylinder — using the point you have marked as the centre.

■ Form the sides of the cylinder by joining the two circles with 45° parallel lines.

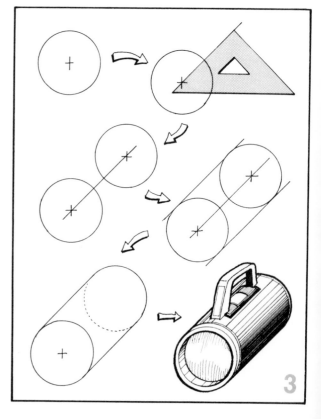

The Isometric View

The *isometric view* is another form of pictorial drawing which can be made with the help of drawing instruments. You may not always need a set square and tee square to produce an isometric view, but they will help you when you first begin to draw using this method.

Unlike perspective views, no vanishing points are used in an isometric drawing. The height, width and length are shown as parallel sets of lines, and can be drawn to actual scale (figure 27:1). In an isometric view, the object is drawn at an angle, with one corner of the object being the closest point to the viewer.

■ All vertical (upright) lines on the object will remain as vertical lines on the drawing.
■ All lines which are horizontal on the object will be drawn at 30° to the horizontal on the paper.

Figure 27

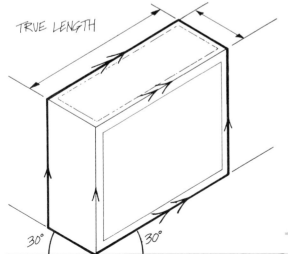

TRUE LENGTH

30°   30°

1

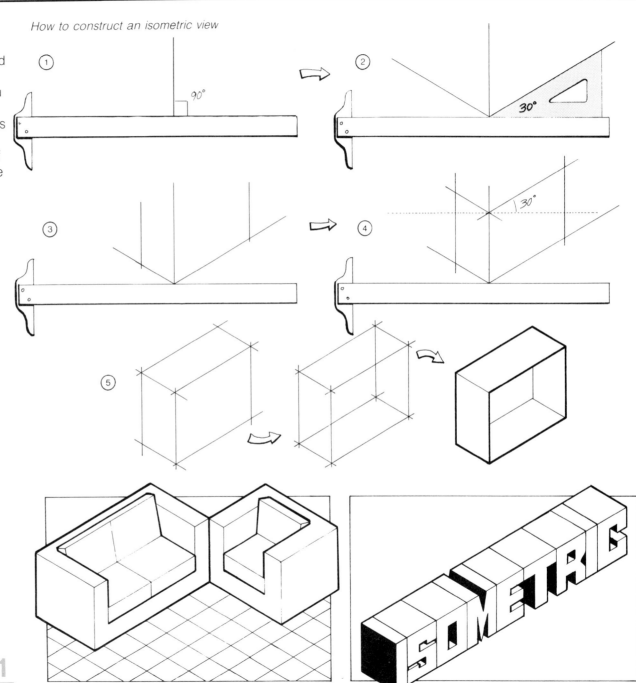

How to construct an isometric view

The Planometric View

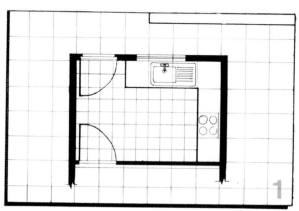

Figure 28

Planometric views are widely used to show buildings or room interiors. This is because they can be easily drawn from a ground plan (a view looking directly down). By extending parallel lines from the ground plan, we can produce a 3-dimensional view.

■ Draw the plan to its true shape and scale (figure 28:1).
■ Rotate the plan so it is at an angle. The commonest angles used are 45°/45° or 30°/60° (figure 28:2).
■ Draw vertical height lines from all important or interesting points on the plan such as the corners of the room or furniture (figure 28:3).

■ If the vertical height lines are drawn to their full-scale length, they will appear too long. Therefore, you must shorten the height lines by ¾ or ⅔ of the scale (figure 28:4).
■ Any circles (or curves) which face upwards on the plan can be drawn as true circles rather than ellipses (figure 28:5).

Draw a plan of an interesting corner of the workshop or design office. From this, produce a planometric view.

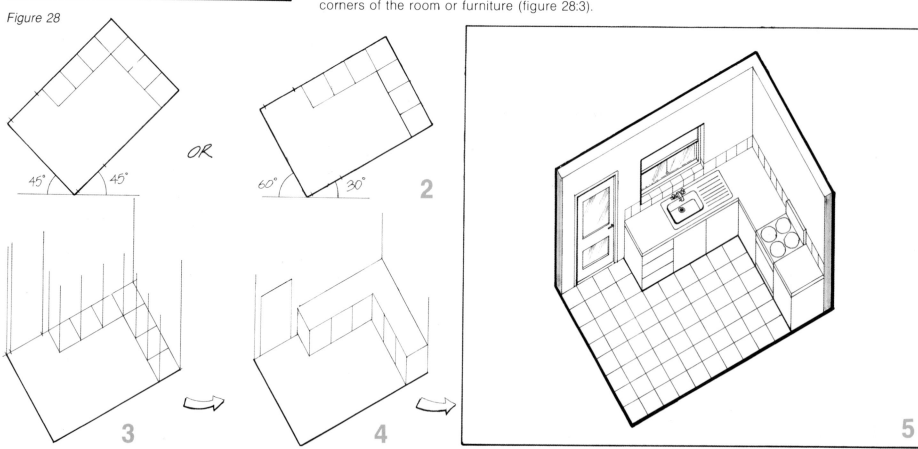

Crating 1

You may have wondered why the previous pages show so many different ways to draw a box! A box or crate can be used as the basis for drawing many other items. This method of drawing is called *crating*. The best way to start is to imagine that the object you wish to draw is packed inside a box or crate.

When you have decided on a suitable viewpoint, the box is lightly drawn in to the correct size and shape. The details of the object can be added, using guidelines where necessary.

Study the room in which you are sitting. Can you list six items that would fit easily into a box shape? Draw three of them using the crating method.

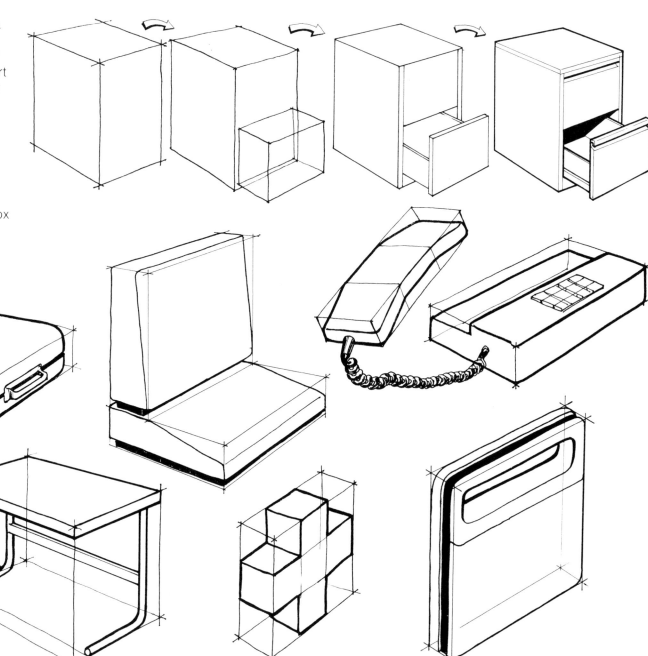

Crating 2

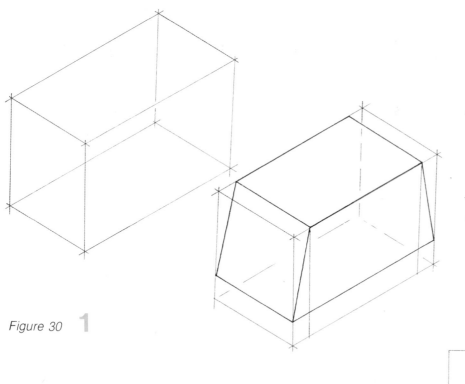

Figure 30 **1**

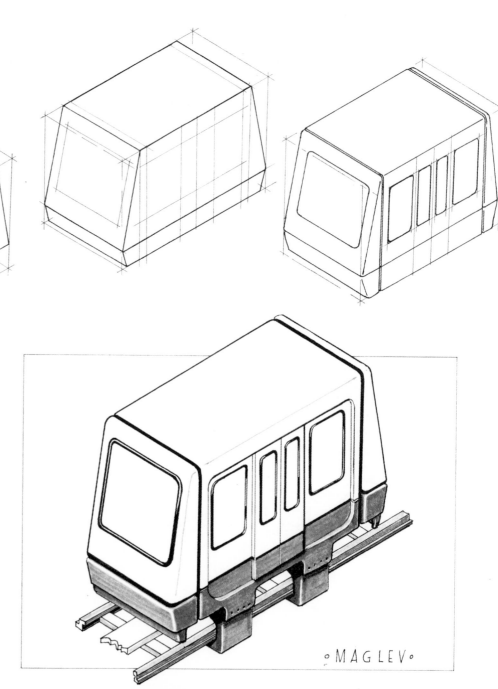

°MAGLEV°

If you look at the series of drawings on this page, you will see that the drawing of the magnetic levitation train (maglev) has been gradually built up from a simple box (figure 30:1). This box has been drawn as an isometric view, but any method of pictorial drawing can be used (see page 17).

(a) Make a drawing of the maglev using the crating method. You could try using a different viewpoint to the one shown.

(b) Use this method to draw some simple objects from your workshop, design office or from home. Draw them as isometric views.

Figure 31

When a circle is tilted in any direction, the shape that we see is always an oval or an *ellipse*. When viewed front-on, it is seen as a true circle. When we begin to tilt it, the whole circle flattens out until it eventually appears as a straight line (see figure 31:1). It is difficult to draw a well proportioned ellipse freehand. Guide lines will help you obtain a better shape (figure 31:2).

In figure 31:3, a circle is drawn in a square which is the front face of a cube. You will notice that the circle touches the square in only four places. The points of contact are half way along each side of the square. In this drawing the circle is a true circle and could be drawn with a compass. However, you could not use a compass to draw a circle on the sides of the cube. The sides appear distorted because this is a pictorial view, and therefore the circles will appear distorted also. They will be seen as ellipses. The ellipses can be sketched using the same four plotting points, at positions half way along each side. (See figure 31:4.) Shapes based on cylinders can be drawn using this method of sketching ellipses, with crating.

■ Draw a pictorial view of a square ended crate.
■ Mark off the half way points on each side of the squares.
■ Sketch in the ellipses using these points as a guide.
■ Complete the object by drawing in the sides (figure 31:5).

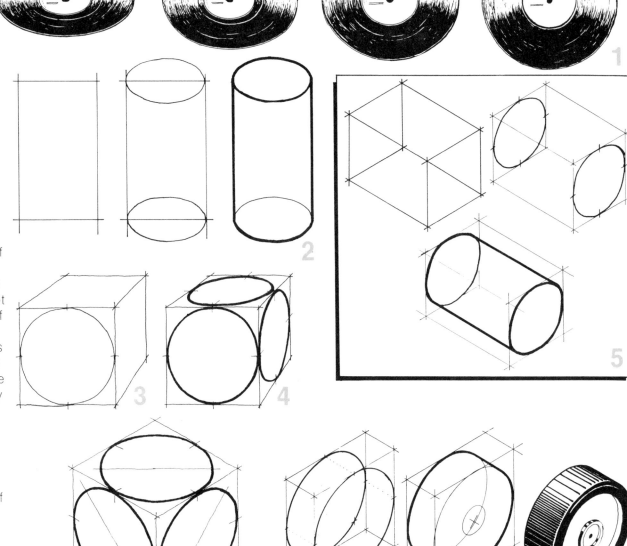

Constructing Ellipses

The techniques for drawing ellipses described on page 31 are suitable for quick design sketches. For a more accurate curve or ellipses, you will need to use a method which gives more points to help you draw your ellipse.

These methods of producing ellipses can be used for a number of different types of pictorial view.

Figure 32:1 shows a cube drawn as an isometric view. To draw a circle on one of the faces of the cube we will need to construct an ellipse, as the angle of view will distort the shape of the circle.

In order to plot the ellipse accurately, we must first draw a flat view of the circle. This method is suitable for isometric and oblique views.

■ Draw the circle (actual size) within a square, with centre lines at right angles (figure 32:2).
■ Draw a number of equally spaced vertical parallel lines across the box. The more lines that you draw, the more plotting points will be created (figure 32:3).
■ Draw the same number of parallel lines onto the face of the cube (figure 32:4).
■ Each line on the flat view is now measured to find the distance from the centre line to where it cuts the circle (figure 32:5). This can be done with a compass or dividers.
■ Transfer the measurements onto the isometric view (figure 32:6).
■ Join up the points (freehand) to form an ellipse on the isometric view (fig. 32:7).

The eight-point method

An alternative way of drawing an ellipse uses eight plotting points (figure 32:8).

■ Draw the full-size circle within a square
■ Draw diagonal lines from corner to corner.
■ Draw vertical and horizontal lines where the diagonals cut the circle.
■ Draw the box as it would appear in perspective or oblique etc.
■ Position diagonal lines on the box as before and transfer the plotting points by measuring or projection.
■ Join up the points using freehand curves to form an ellipse.

This method is suitable for drawing curves and ellipses in perspective views.

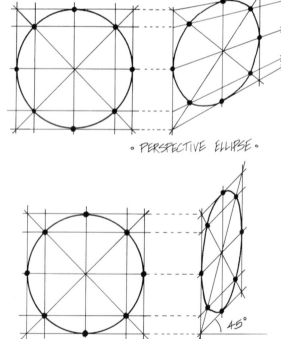

· PERSPECTIVE ELLIPSE ·

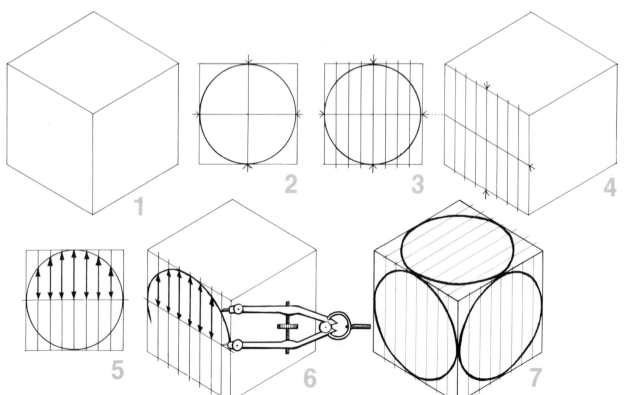

Figure 32   · OBLIQUE ELLIPSE ·   **8**

1 Design the package and cover for a new computer chess game. Use either a one-point or two-point perspective view of the board and some chess pieces as the basis for your cover design (see pages 20-24).

2 The first prize in a competition is the chance to win your own 'dream' bedroom. Imagine that you have won this competition. Prepare some designs for the room of your choice. Show the room as either:
(i)   a perspective view, or
(ii) an isometric view, or
(iii) a planometric view.

   Show suggested colour schemes and collect fabric samples to make the presentation more effective.

3 Draw an isometric view of a workbench or table. Include in your design provision for:
(i)   storage for drawing materials
(ii) a temporary drawing surface.

4 Produce three design sketches for a picnic table. Remember, it must be transportable and easily assembled. Use the crating method of drawing (see pages 29-30).

5 Design a unit that will house two small animals such as hamsters or mice. Consider the animals' needs for sleeping, eating and exercise areas. Draw a dimensioned plan view, and from this, produce a planometric view of the unit. (See page 28.)

6 You are required to design a 'desk-tidy' using several sections of PVC tube. The diameters of the tubes vary. Draw three different arrangements as isometric views, constructing the ellipses with care. (See pages 31 and 32.)

7 (a) Draw a cylinder as an isometric view and use the shape you have created as the basis for the design of a small aluminum container. The top is to be turned from hardwood.

   (b) Using geometric shapes produce ideas for a surface pattern that would be suitable for etching or engraving onto the aluminium. (See pages 31, 32 and 14.)

8 Figure 33:1 shows a kitchen drawn as an isometric view. A disabled person would find it difficult to cope with the normal fixtures and fittings of a kitchen such as this, which has been designed for able-bodied persons.

   (a) Study the kitchen carefully and identify the problems that a person in a wheelchair would face.

   (b) Re-design the kitchen so that it would be more suitable for use by a person in a wheelchair. Draw your solution as an isometric view. (See page 27.)

Figure 33   *Kitchen design: drawn as an isometric view*

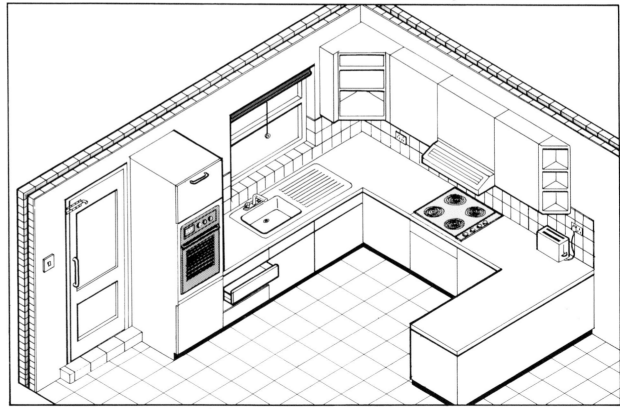

Light and Shade

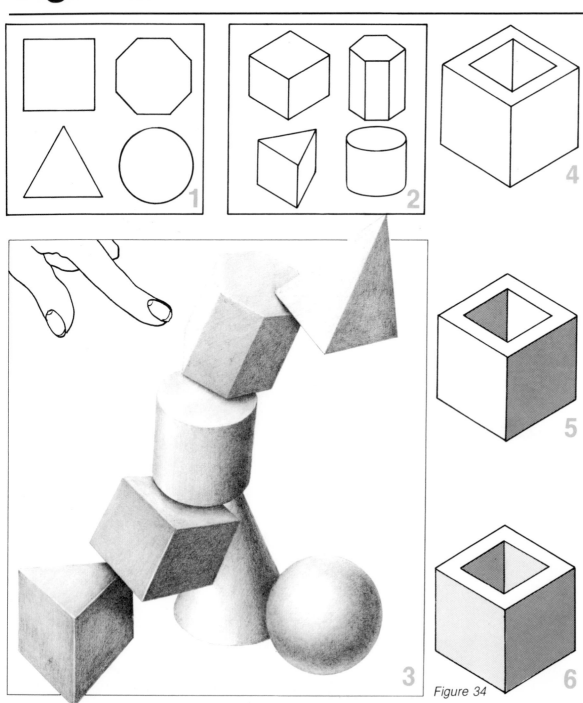

Figure 34

Simple line drawings can record and describe design ideas. Outlines are enough to show flat shapes (figure 34:1). Pictorial sketches use lines to show the framework of a solid shape (figure 34:2). These lines give enough information to tell us what an object is. However, the lines in these drawings only show the edges of an object and where surfaces meet. In reality, we cannot see these lines on objects. We notice that one surface is darker than another, because of the effects of light and shade.

Tone

If an object is placed close to a window in daylight, the side facing the window will appear to be a much lighter colour than the side which is in shade, facing away from the light. These lighter and darker versions of the same colour are referred to as *tones*. By shading a drawing with different tones, you can make the objects look more solid. In figure 34:3 the graduation of tones (the gradual change between light and dark) on the cylinder and sphere make their surfaces appear curved.

Contrast

The difference between light and dark tones is called *contrast*. An object with one tone all over has no contrast. It looks flat and and dull (figure 34:4). In figure 34:5, a dramatic high contrast effect has been created by using two contrasting tones — very dark and very light. Figure 34:6 is a more natural view, because light, dark and medium tones have been used.

Pencil Shading

Pencil shading is the easiest way of producing tones on a drawing. Careful shading with a pencil can create realist effects. Many different tones can be made by using one medium grade (HB) pencil. Simply by varying the pressure on the pencil, a very light tone (almost white) or a dark, blackish tone can be achieved. In between these extremes will exist a range of *mid-tones*, which will be different greys.

Copy the range of tones in figure 35:1. The rectangle is divided into eight sections. Use an HB or B pencil to produce each step, from the darkest tone, through grey, to the lightest tone.

This type of shading is used to produce the different tones on the vehicle in figure 35:3 Here each surface is at a different angle and so reflects a different amount of light.

Now try to produce the effect shown in figure 35:2. This time each tone has been gradually lightened. This method of shading is ideal for showing the change of tone on a curved surface, as on the cylinderical shapes is figures 35:3 and 35:4.

Figure 35

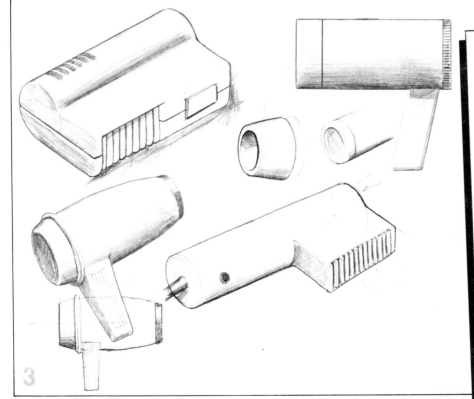

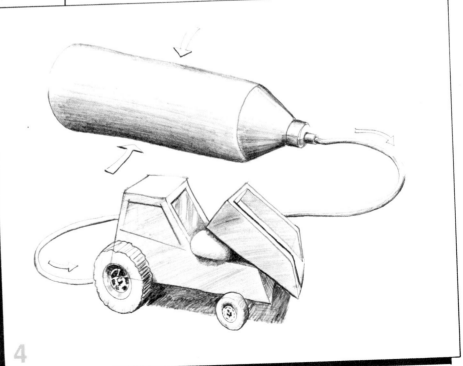

Adding Tone with Lines and Dots

All the drawings on this page have been 'shaded' by using lines or dots. Can you see that when the lines or dots are grouped closely together, dark areas of tone are created? When more space is left between the lines or dots, the tone is lighter.

Some of these techniques are very useful for quick sketches, and can be produced with fine line markers or ball-point pens as well as a pencil.

Dry transfer tone

If you look closely at figure 36:1 you will discover that the tone is made up of tiny dots. These dots are not hand drawn by the designer. Instead he/she has used ready made sheets of printed tone called *dry transfer tone*.

These are transfers of evenly printed dots that form even or graduated tones. Dry transfer tone is rather expensive, but quick to use, and gives crisp, professional results. This method of adding tone is useful for illustrations and charts that need to be photocopied, as it prints well.

How to use dry transfer tone

■ Place the sheet of dry transfer tone over the drawing.
■ Cut out a rough outline, taking care not to cut through the backing sheet.
■ Remove the film from the backing sheet and lay it on the drawing.
■ Cut the outline of the area where the tone is to be added with a sharp blade. (Be careful!) Peel away the unwanted film.
■ To ensure that the remaining film is fixed to the drawing, place the backing sheet over the tone and rub it with a blunt pencil (See fig. 36:2.)

Figure 36

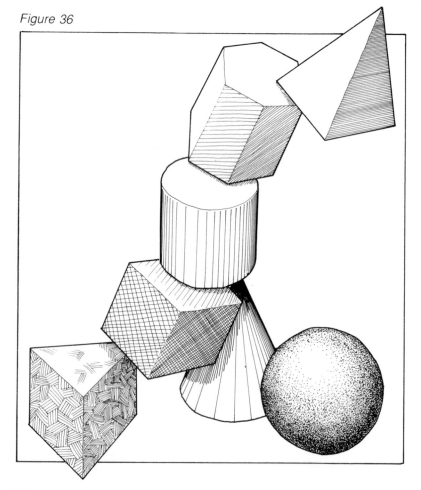

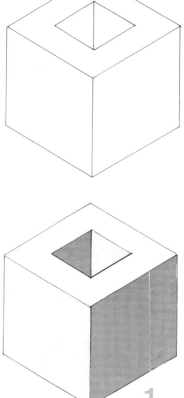

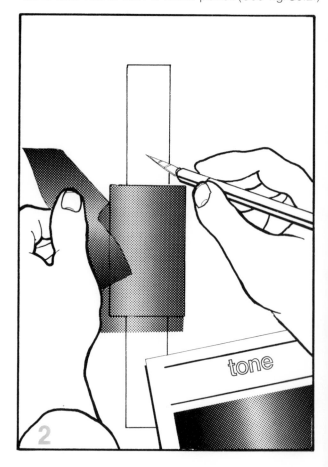

Casting Shadows

In figure 37:1 *shadows* have been added to indicate that a strong light is shining from one side. The areas which are facing away from the light are 'in shade'.

Shadows occur whenever a solid shape blocks the path of light. The rays of light bounce off the shape and an area of dark shadow is produced behind it.

We can use shadows in drawings to increase the feeling of depth, and to suggest a background for objects. If we follow a few basic guidelines, an estimated shadow should be enough to create the effect we need for most types of design drawing.

Guidelines for drawing shadows

■ The shape of the shadow will depend on the shape which is blocking out the light. Look at the shapes of objects and their shadows on this page. The shadow will be on the side furthest from the light.

■ The position of the shadow will be affected by the position of the light. Notice how the shadow lengthens when the light is in a low position (figure 37:2). What happens to the shadow when the light is high and above the object?

■ The shadow will follow the form of the background (e.g. if the background is curved the shadow cast on its surface will also curve).

■ A shadow is not really black. It is a darker tone of the surface on which it falls (e.g. a shadow falling on a red background will be a dark red). In black and white drawings the shadows can be made very dark. (See figure 37:3.)

■ Remember that shadows can also be cast inside hollow objects and underneath ledges. (See figure 37:4).

Figure 37

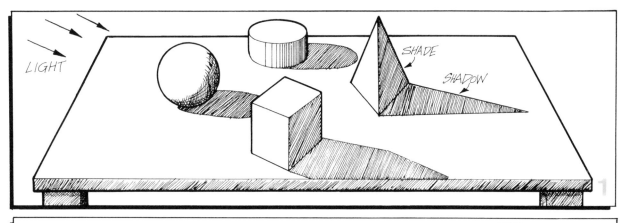

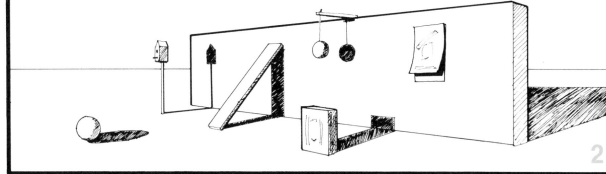

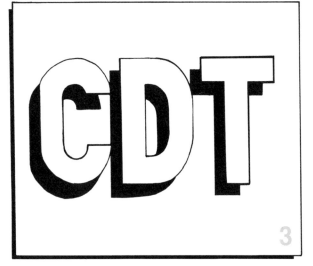

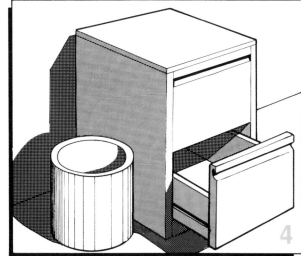

Constructing Shadows

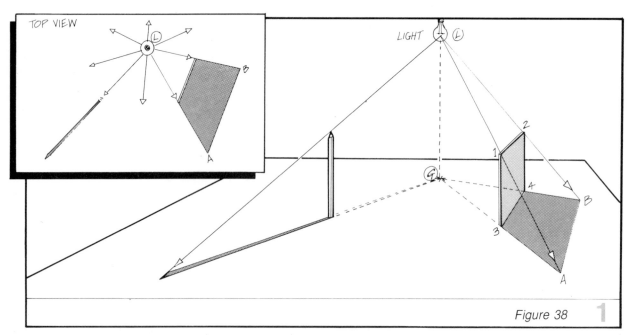

Flat shapes

If you need to draw accurate shadows you can use the following method (see figure 38:1):

■ Imagine that the light (L) comes from one point on a lamp, and that rays of light fan out from that point.
■ Mark the point (G) on the ground directly below the light (L).
■ Draw lines from (L) through the top corners of the shapes (points 1 and 2).
■ Now draw lines from (G) through the bottom corners of the shapes (points 3 and 4).
■ Mark where the two sets of lines cross. We will call these A and B. These points will form the corners of the shadow.
■ Join up A and B to complete the outline of the cast shadow. You can shade this in.

Figure 38 **1**

Solids

Figure (38:2) shows how to find the shadow cast by a solid cube. This is basically the same as the above method for a flat rectangle. However, this shape has more corners and so there are more points to plot.

Some of the shadow and the points, will be hidden from view. It is still important to show them on the drawing so that the shadow may be constructed accurately.

■ Vertical lines are drawn from the points on the curve to the base of the shape (ground level).
■ Lines from G are drawn through the base points.
■ Where they intersect the lines from L. the outlines of the shadow can be drawn in freehand.

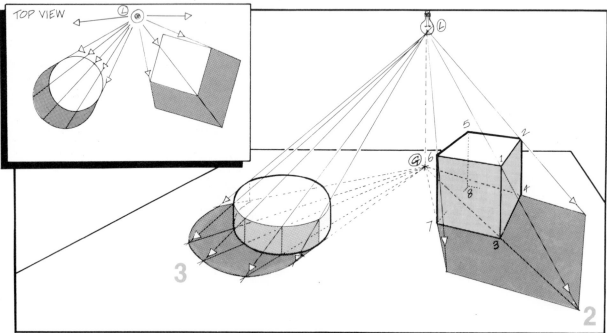

Reflections and Highlights

Reflections

Look at the photograph in figure 39:1. Can you see the reflections in the glass table top? All shiny surfaces will reflect light from their surroundings. If we wish to show smooth or shiny material in a drawing we must indicate these reflections. Figures 39:2 and 39:3 show illustrations of bathroom mirrors. The reflections have been sketched in to give an impression of the shiny mirror surface. Notice how the reflected objects and the real objects are opposite each other and appear to be equal distances apart (figure 39:2). It is not always necessary to make a detailed drawing of a reflection. A few simple lines are often enough to suggest a reflected image. (See figure 39:4.)

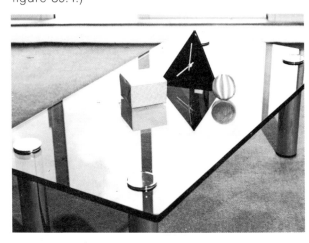

Figure 39   1

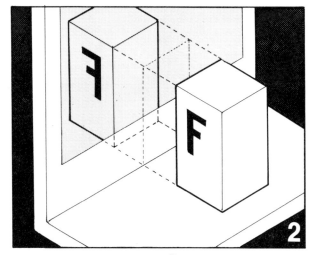

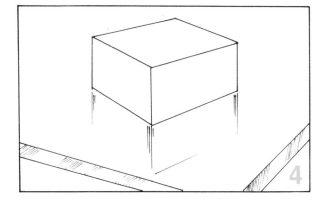

Highlights

We particularly notice highlights when light is reflected off a surface or the edge of an object. This is the type of reflection which is most used in design illustration. Realism can be added to a drawing by using highlights. Designers use simple techniques (shown below) to show these highlights on different shaped objects.

■ A flat, horizontal surface always has reflections and highlights that are vertical to the eye.

■ Curved forms such as cylinders distort reflections and stretch them along the length of the object. When adding reflections to a cylinder or tube it is best to position them to the left or right of the centre. This makes the drawing look more interesting. On a tube the inside surface can also reflect. This will be directly opposite the reflection on the outside.

■ The 'window' reflection is a very popular way of showing a highlight on a sphere.

■ Highlights are often placed on the edges of objects. They are used to create a three-dimensional effect.

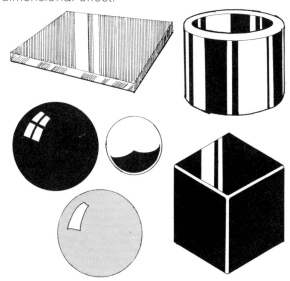

Drawing with Basic Forms

It is easier to shade complicated objects if you simplify them into basic forms, such as cubes, spheres, cylinders, etc. The toys on this page are made up of very simple forms that have been added together to give an overall shape. What are the basic solid shapes that have been used in the objects on this page? The toys have been drawn with light shining from one direction. However, if you look carefully you will notice that one of the shadows has been drawn incorrectly. Can you spot the deliberate mistake?

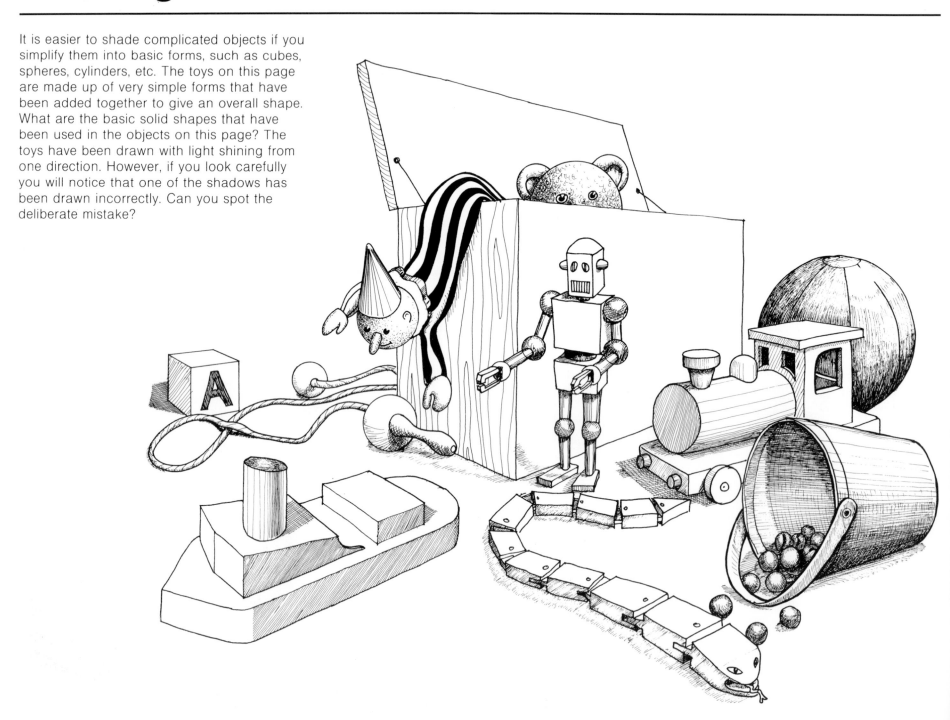

Texture and Materials

Shiny — rough — smooth — soft. What do these words describe? All these words describe the look or feel of the surface of something — its *texture*. In figure 41:1 different types of marks have been drawn onto the cubes to give an impression of different textures. Some appear to have rough surfaces while others look smooth or shiny. We are able to see texture because of the effect of light and shade on the object. If you look closely at a rough surface, you will discover that it is covered in tiny lumps. It is the shadows cast by these lumps that make the texture easy to see. On a surface which has many small dents, like expanded polystyrene or a sponge, the shadows will be cast in the hollows. The textures on the cubes in figure 41:1 have been produced using lines and dots which imitate the grouping of shadows, patterns and reflections on different materials.

It is important to show texture in design drawings. Not only does it make them more interesting to look at, it also shows the material that you are intending to use in your finished design.

Figure 41:2 shows a range of different textures. Can you see how the effects have been achieved? For example, one has been produced by placing paper over a textured surface and rubbing lightly with a pencil or crayon.

■ Choose three of the textures in figure 41:2 and try to produce a similar effect.
■ Create three interesting textures of your own using dots, lines, or rubbing.
■ Experiment with a range of drawing materials such as charcoal, ball point pens and markers, to achieve different texture effects.

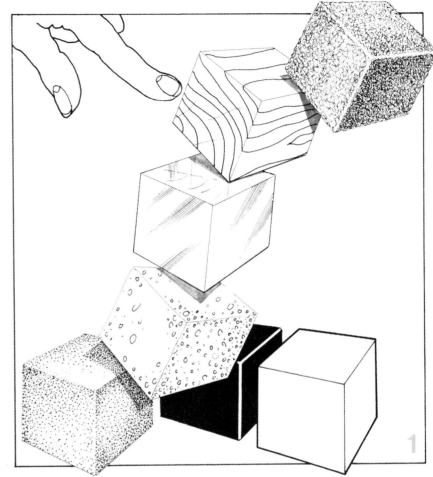

Figure 41

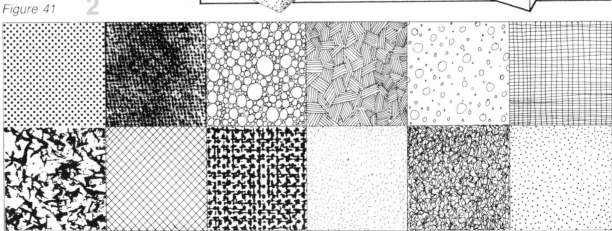

Coarse Textures

The chairs drawn on this page appear to be made from materials having a coarse or rough surface. Try to imagine how they would feel to the touch. Lines and dots have been used to imitate the surface of these materials. Notice that the texturing has not been applied evenly all over the objects. More texturing has been applied in certain areas to show the effects of light and shade. The surfaces which are shaded from the light have been textured most strongly. Surfaces which face the light have little or no texture drawn on them. If objects are textured evenly they tend to look flat.

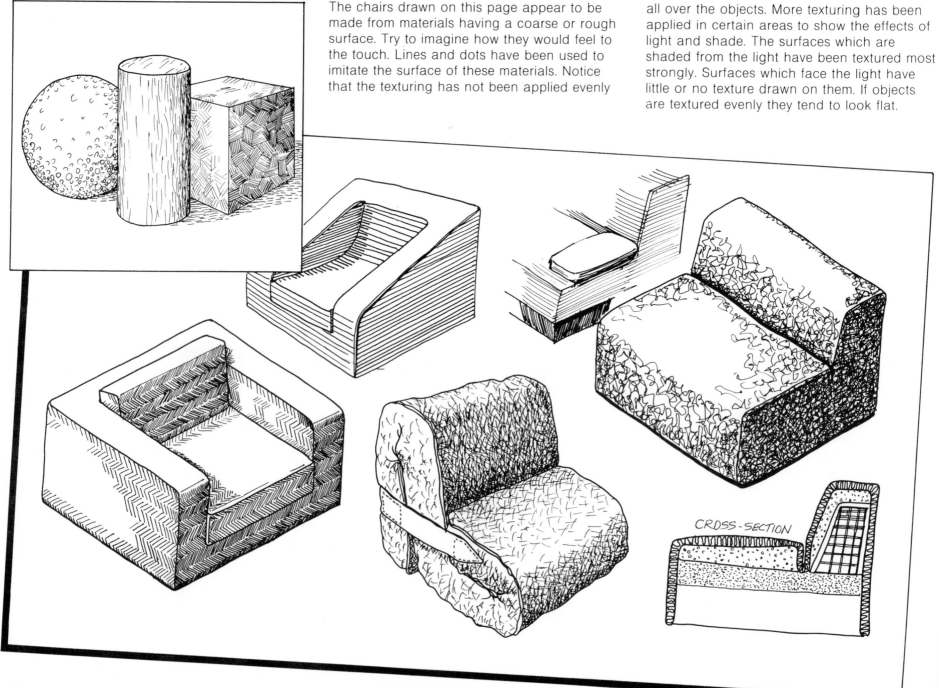

CROSS-SECTION

Shiny Surfaces

Materials such as plastics, metal and glass, often have smooth shiny surfaces. It is the highlights and reflections on materials which give them their shiny appearance.

Adding the shine

The simplest way of suggesting a reflection is to draw a number of short parallel lines across a surface.

■ On *horizontal* surfaces, such as the table top, these lines should be drawn *vertically* (figure 43:1).

■ On *vertical* surfaces, such as the mirror, the lines should be drawn *diagonally* (figure 43:2).

■ The table in figure 43:3 has been made to look as if the surface is polished. Highlights have been indicated by removing areas of shading from the drawing with an eraser.

■ On very shiny surfaces such as chromium-plated steel, reflections will appear as high contrast areas of dark and light (figure 43:4).

■ If you use a dark background paper, and draw in the highlights with a white pastel or pencil crayon, you an achieve a very dramatic effect (figure 43:5).

■ If the material you are drawing is transparent as well as shiny — such as glass or clear acrylic — you wil need to suggest the shapes that you can see through it. Much of the detail will be lost, so only a thin broken line need be used for any outlines of shapes or edges beyond (figure 43:6).

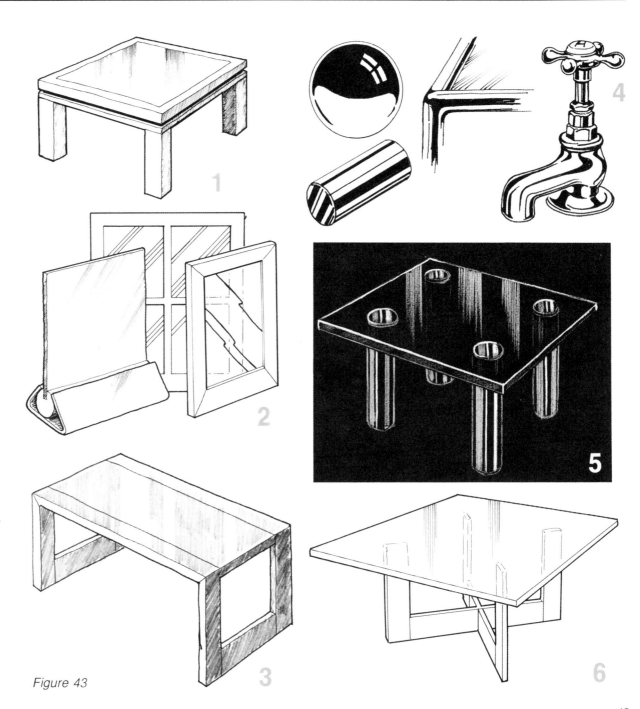

Figure 43

Matt Surfaces

Some materials feel quite smooth or have only a dull surface sheen. This type of surface which has an extremely fine texture is described as *matt*. Materials which are often given a matt texture include paper, card, rubber, metals, wood and plastics.

If you look at the drawings on this page you will notice that the tone has been applied evenly. This gives an impression of a matt finish. All high contrast shading and reflections have been left out, and highlights are softer.

We can recognise different types of wood by studying the patterns formed by the grain. A simple method of showing wood on a drawing is to use lines or shading to suggest this grain. It is not necessary to cover the whole object in grain lines. In figure 44:1 why do you think most lines have been applied to the side facing away from the light?

Careful pencil shading can be used to create a smooth surface. You will notice in figure 44:2 that there are no obvious pencil marks which might suggest a texture. Tones change from light to dark very gradually, suggesting a smooth matt surface.

In figure 44:3 a soft sheen has been added to this marker drawing. This effect was achieved by smudging chalk onto the areas facing the light.

Evenly spaced lines can be used instead of pencil shading. By altering the distance between the lines a lighter or darker tone is created. In figure 44:4 you will see that only a few lines have been drawn on the lightest parts of the object. When the lines are drawn with a ruler a 'hard' effect is created. This is especially useful for showing materials such as metal and plastics.

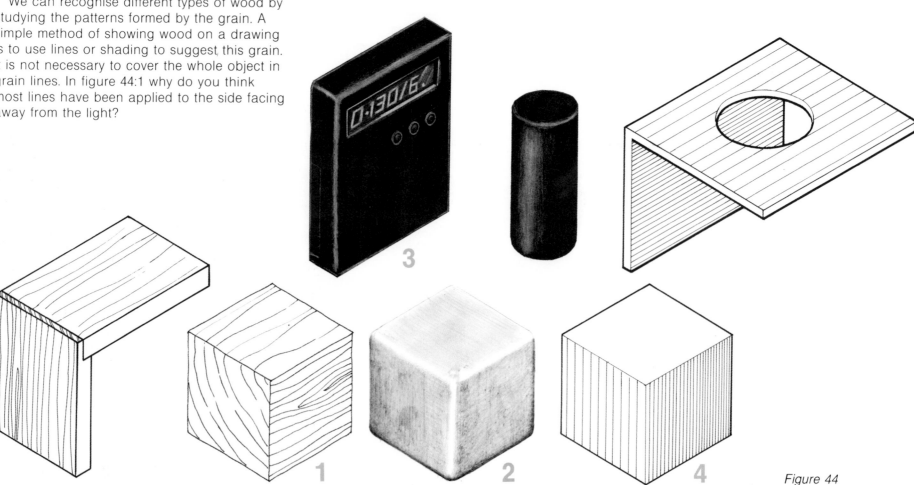

Figure 44

Assignments 3

1 Make sketches for the design of an adjustable mirror. The design is to be based on a mirror tile 150 × 150 mm. You must illustrate clearly the materials in your design. (See pages 39 and 41–44).

2 Draw six cubes, approximately 50 mm high. Apply surface textures so that each cube appears to be made from one of the materials from the list below:
(i) concrete,
(ii) pine,
(iii) polished aluminium,
(iv) a coarse fabric such as hessian or corduroy,
(v) expanded polystyrene,
(vi) transparent acrylic.

3 Design a candleholder based on the theme of 'interlocking shapes'. Your design should hold at least five candles. It should be suitable for casting in aluminium, and have a highly polished finish. Use reflections and highlights on your drawings to show this finish.

4 You are given the workings of a mechanical toy robot. Design a body for the robot that will appeal to a young child. In your drawing, try to make the robot look metallic. Use basic geometric forms to help you in your design, for example cubes, cones, spheres, and cylinders. (See pages 40, 39 and 43.)

5 You have been asked to arrange the lighting in a scene from a horror film. If the light is low, large menacing shadows will be cast.
(a) Draw the stage set.
(b) Place a figure in the set and draw in the shadows it will cast onto the background.
(c) Indicate the position of the light source.

6 Develop ideas for a 'touch' toy or game to be used by visually handicapped young people. Your design should be based on either:
(i) shapes
(ii) textures
Use drawing techniques which clearly show the solid forms or surface textures you intend to use.

7 A maze is a complicated network of paths or passages designed to puzzle those who walk through it. Figure 45:1 shows a drawing of the centre of a maze.
(a) Using this as a guide, design a maze of your own. The size of the maze will only be limited by the size of the paper you draw on.
(b) Shade your maze by using dry transfer tone as in figure 45:1, or use a pencil to create a similar tonal effect. (See pages 25, 34, 35 and 36.)

Figure 45

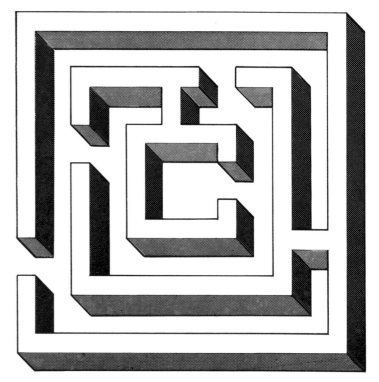

Orthographic Projection 1

Once a solution to a design problem has been decided on, a *working drawing* must be made. This working drawing will need to show all the dimensions and details necessary for the object (or its component parts) to be made *exactly* as the designer requires. To avoid the distortions of shape and size which often occur on pictorial views (page 17) a series of flat, square-on views are drawn. These views are known as *Orthographic views* (figure 46:1).

When these orthographic views are drawn together in a related group, they are called orthographic projections. There are two different types of orthographic projection. These are called first-angle projection and third-angle projection.

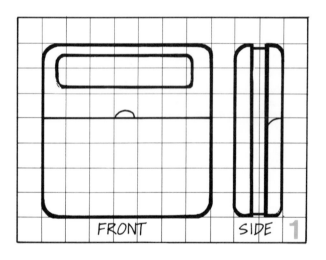

When drawing an orthographic projection, we refer to each view as:

■ *the plan*. This is the view looking directly down onto the object.
■ *the front elevation*. This is usually the view that shows the most information.
■ *the end elevation*. This is either (or both) of the remaining side views.

First angle projection

Imagine that the object you wish to draw is suspended in a box. Each elevation can be drawn onto the side of the box. These views are obtained by looking at the object in the direction of the arrows shown in figure 46:2 (P, F and E).

These views are projected right *through* the object onto the inside of the box, almost as if they were shadows. If the box is then opened out, the three views appear as shown in figure 46:3. This is how you should set out your drawing for a *first-angle,* orthographic projection.

Start by drawing the front view. The plan view is placed below the front view. If the right-hand view of the object is to be drawn, it is placed to the left of the front view. (The left-hand view is drawn to the right of the front view.)

Any Drawing made using this method must include the British Standards 308 symbol for first-angle projection shown in figure 46:4.

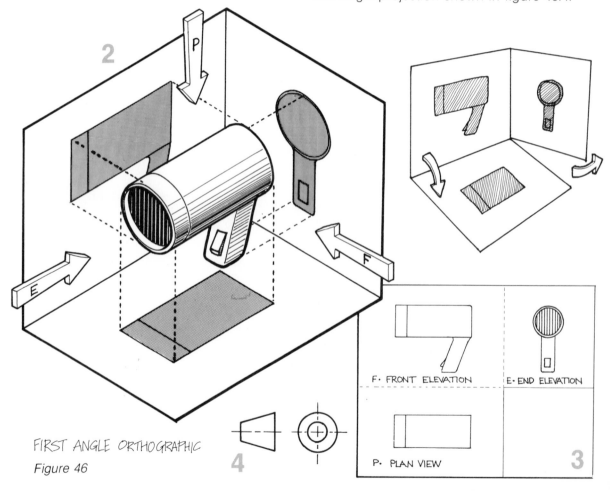

FIRST ANGLE ORTHOGRAPHIC
Figure 46

Third-angle projection

Third-angle projection is an alternative method of arranging orthographic (flat) views of an object.

In third angle, we again imagine that the object is suspended in a box. However, this time we assume that the box is transparent. If you imagine that you are looking through the box at the object, the view that you would see is drawn onto the sides of the box (figure 47:1). If the box is opened out, the three views will appear as shown in figure 47:2.

Notice that the plan view is above the front view, and the left hand view is placed to the left of the front view. This is how you should set out your drawing for a third-angle orthographic projection.

Any drawing made using this method must include the British Standards symbol for third-angle projection shown in figure 47:3.

■ If the object you are drawing is complicated or is made up of many different parts, you may need to show more than three views. It is important to draw these views in relation to each other.

■ Dimensions and notes about materials, construction etc., can be added to your drawing. (See page 48.)

■ Hidden details can be shown by using dotted lines.

■ An orthographic drawing can be used as the basis of a presentation drawing. This can be very effective when drawn on coloured paper. (See pages 81–82.)

■ The addition of a pictorial view may help to give a clearer impression of the finished design.

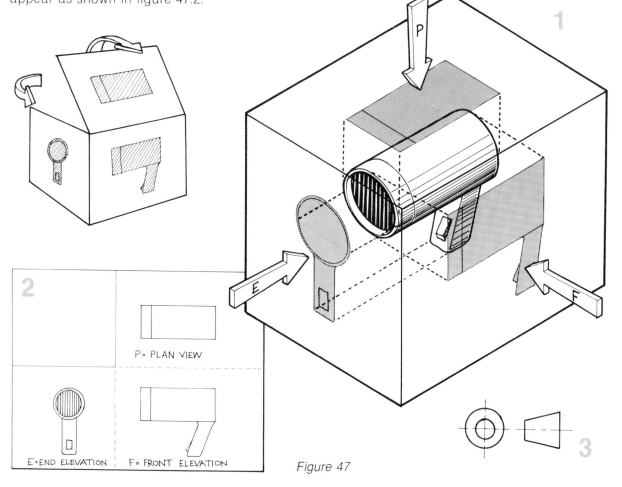

P○ PLAN VIEW

E○END ELEVATION   F○FRONT ELEVATION

Figure 47

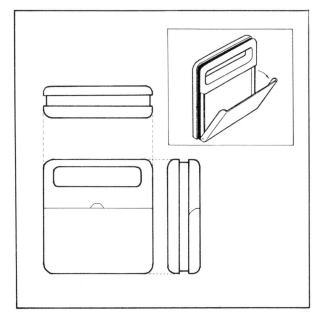

Lines and Conventions

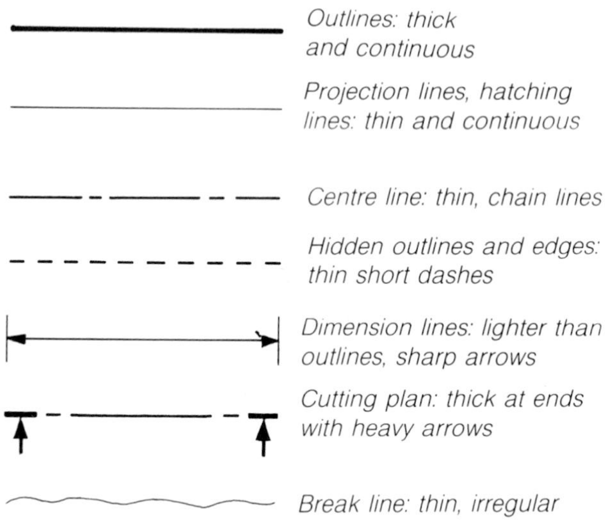

Outlines: thick and continuous

Projection lines, hatching lines: thin and continuous

Centre line: thin, chain lines

Hidden outlines and edges: thin short dashes

Dimension lines: lighter than outlines, sharp arrows

Cutting plan: thick at ends with heavy arrows

Break line: thin, irregular

Figure 48 **1**

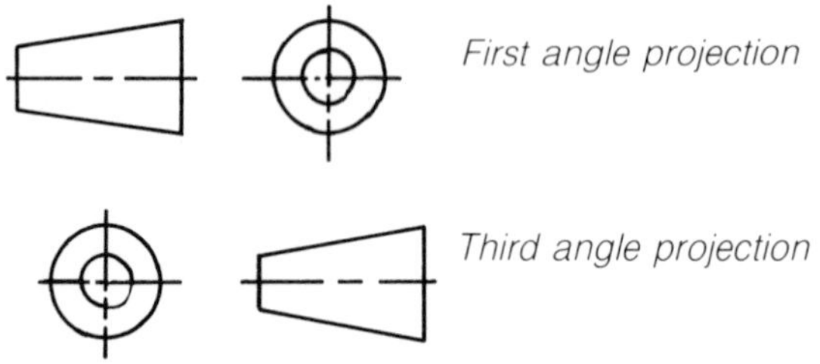

First angle projection

Third angle projection

A working drawing must show all the dimensions and details needed for an object to be made exactly as the designer requires. This information must be accurate. Any lines, symbols or abbreviations should be clear and easy to understand. To avoid confusion, it is important that the same symbols and lines are used by everybody. The British Standards Institution recommends particular ways of showing information on a drawing. This standardize use of symbols and lines is called a *drawing convention*. These conventions are recognized and understood all over the world. The examples from British Standards publications shown below can be useful in the preparation of working drawings. For greater detail, refer to British Standards 308 or PD. 7308 (Engineering Drawing Practice for Schools and Colleges).

Dimensions

When we put *dimensions* on a drawing, we show the measurements on it. On a working drawing you will need to show all the dimensions that are necessary to make your design.

■ A dimension should be shown only once on a drawing.
■ Position the dimension lines well away from the outline of the object to avoid confusion. The dimensions should be placed so that they can be read from the bottom or right-hand side of the drawing.
■ You should not need to turn the paper around in order to read the dimensions.
■ All figures should be placed above but not on the dimension line.
■ Use neat, clean, sharp arrow heads. The arrow head should touch the projection line or limiting line.

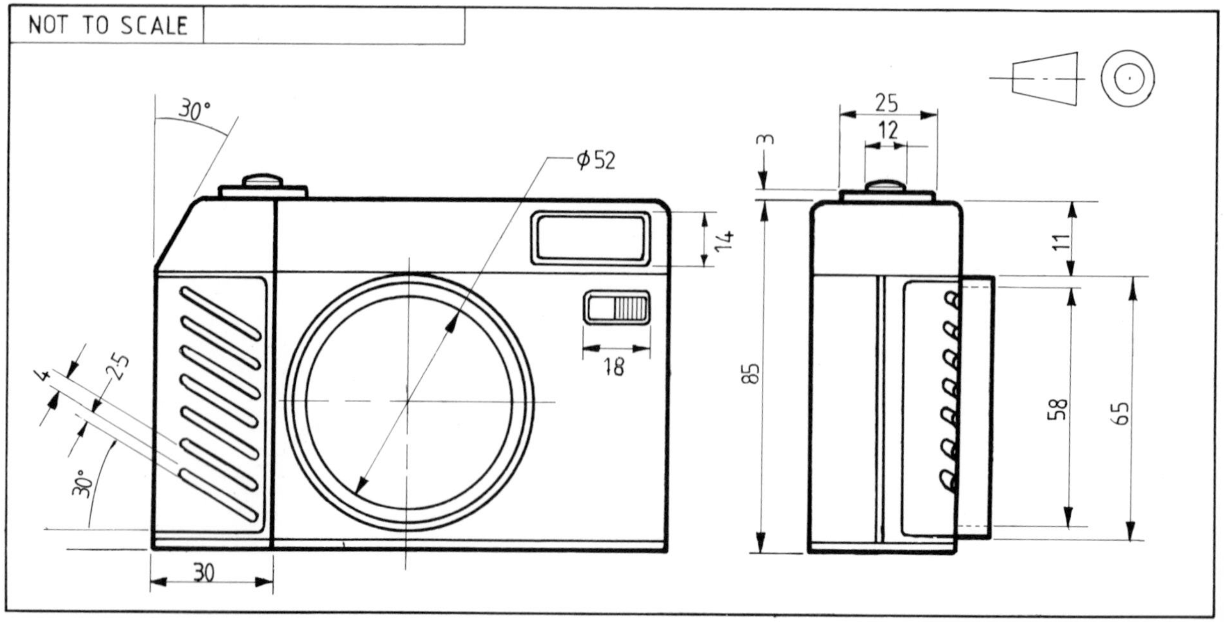

Line

Each type of line has its own special meaning and use. Figure 48:1 shows how and where each type of line is used.

The Sectional View

Sometimes we need to make a drawing that shows the details hidden inside an object. To do this it is useful to imagine that the object has been cut through or *sectioned*.

The sectional view in figure 49:2 shows the object of figure 49:1 as if it has been sliced through. This drawing shows the inside of the object, the thickness of the construction material, and gives a clue as to how it has been made. Figure 49:3 is called a *cross-section*. The section has been drawn as a flat view and shows the true shape at that position.

The line along which the object is sectioned is called the *cutting plane*. The position of the cutting plane should be shown on another view using a *section line*. Arrows are used at the end of these lines, pointing in the direction in which the object is viewed (figure 49:1). These lines should be labelled AA, BB etc.

- Notice that the exposed, cut surfaces have been shown by *hatching* with thin, parallel lines, drawn at an angle of 45°. To avoid confusion where two surfaces meet, the lines are drawn in the oposite direction.
- Cuts may be on horizontal or vertical planes (figure 49:4).
- In engineering drawings, nuts, bolts, rivets, ribs, etc. are not shown sectioned along their length and so are not hatched.
- If the object is symmetrical, only half of the object need be shown as a section (figure 49:5).

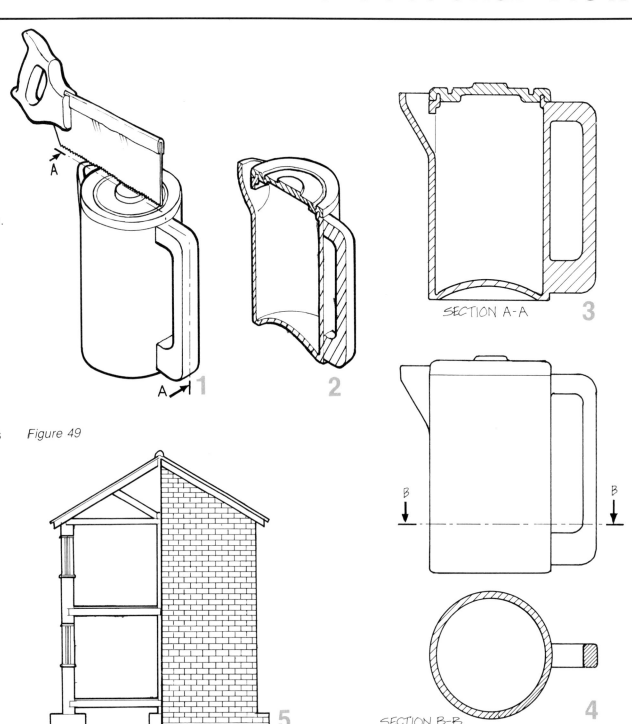

Figure 49

SECTION A-A

SECTION B-B

49

Hidden Details

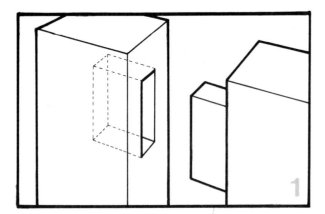

Hidden details as the name suggests, are parts of an object which cannot normally be seen. If we could see these parts it would be easier to understand how an object is made or how it works. There are a number of ways that we can show these hidden details on a drawing.

■ Dotted lines can be added to a drawing to show the outline of the shapes inside an object (figure 50:1).
■ We can imagine that the skin of the object is transparent so we can see inside (figure 50:2).
■ An object can be drawn as if layers have been removed to show the construction beneath the surface (figure 50:3).
■ Part of the outer skin or case may be drawn as if it has been sliced or cut away to show the inside (figure 50:4).

Figure 50

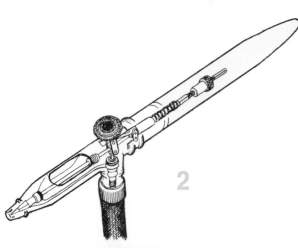

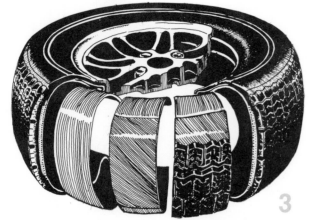

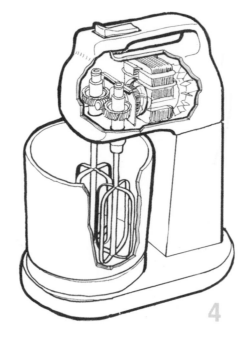

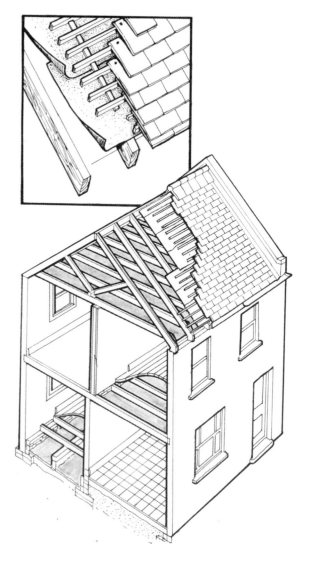

Use a suitable method for showing hidden details in one of the following items:
(i)   a dowel joint,
(ii)   a torch
(iii) an electric kettle.

Thick and Thin Lines

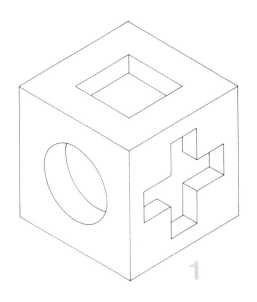

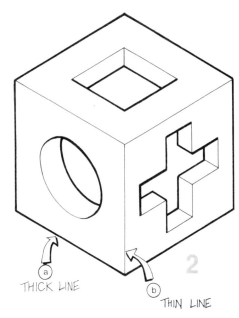

THICK LINE

THIN LINE

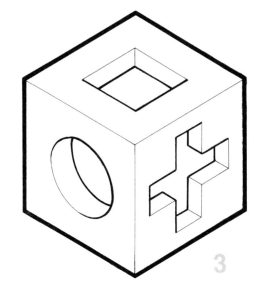

Figure 51

Compare the two drawings of the cube in figures 51:1 and 51:2. One of the drawings has been greatly improved by the addition of thicker lines. This technique is a simple method of giving a pictorial drawing impact. The thick lines create a shadow effect which makes the object appear more solid. Thick and thin lines are often used by technical illustrators, especially for drawings in manuals and instruction leaflets.

Some simple rules can be used to help us decide where to use the thicker lines.

■ A *thick* line is added to an edge where only one surface is seen (figure 51:2 a).
■ A line which shows two surfaces meeting on an edge is drawn *thin* (figure 51:2b).
■ For added impact an even thicker line is drawn around the outline of the object (figure 51:3).

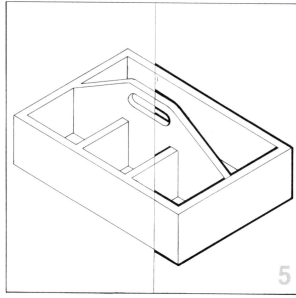

Draw an englarged view of fig 51:5 above (using a grid if you wish — see page 55). Complete the thick lines where necessary.

51

Exploded Views

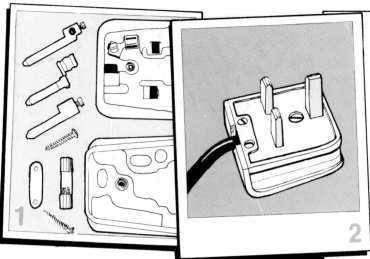

Figure 52

Figure 52:1 is a picture of all the different components (parts) which together make up a 3-pin plug. Would you find it easy to re-assemble these components if you had never seen a plug before?

Figure 52:2 shows a view of the assembled plug. However, this drawing does not show clearly the way in which the components are assembled. In order to show *how* and *where* these components fit together we can use a technique called *exploded drawing*. (See figure 52:3.)

Although this title suggests an explosion it is truer to say that the drawing shows the object pulled apart. The components are not scattered over the paper, but are laid out in an ordered and linear form (following straight lines).

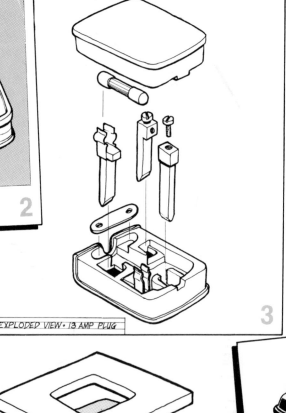

EXPLODED VIEW · 13 AMP PLUG

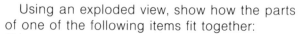

Using an exploded view, show how the parts of one of the following items fit together:
(i)   a pencil sharpener;
(ii) a jewellery box with a tray inside,
(iii) a torch.

Down to the Last Detail

Sometimes, the smaller details on a drawing may be difficult to see and understand. An enlarged view of these details will show them more clearly (figure 53:1).

The magnified drawing is usually shown in a frame. Notice how the frame helps to focus our attention on the detail, and separates it from the rest of the illustration. A circular frame can give you the idea that we are looking through a magnifying glass. These frames can also be used to show methods of construction, e.g. fixings which would not normally be seen. (See figure 53:4.)

Figure 53

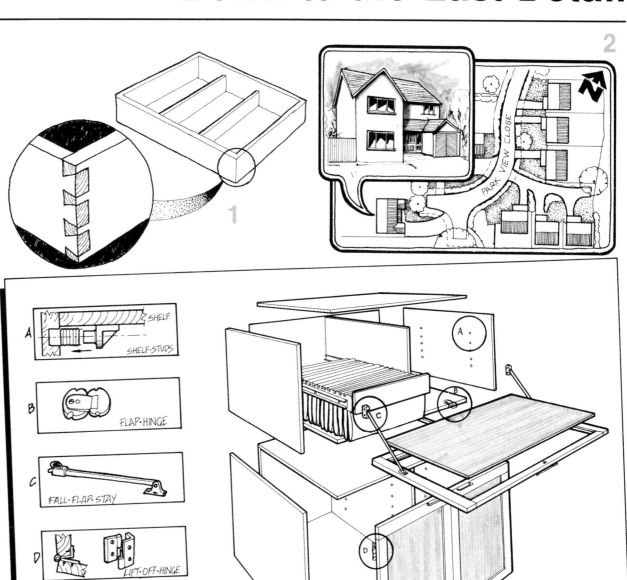

A — SHELF / SHELF·STUDS

B — FLAP·HINGE

C — FALL·FLAP·STAY

D — LIFT·OFF·HINGE

E — PLINTH·FITTING

J. SANDERS | HOME STUDY·OFFICE UNIT | EXPLODED VIEW | DRG. № 12

Drawing with Grids

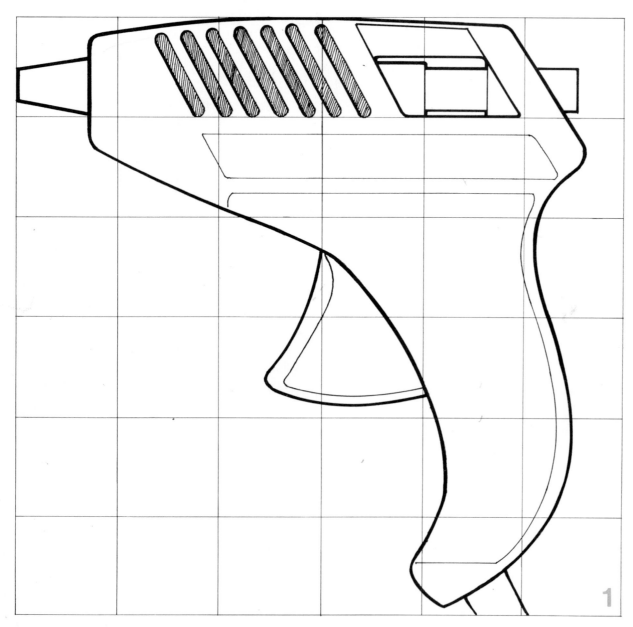

All the drawings on this page have been made with the aid of a *grid*. A grid can be used as a guide, especially if you are drawing freehand. The grid helps you to plot the drawing, because the space is divided into regular areas.

Enlarging and reducing

Sometimes we want to enlarge or reduce the size of a picture. A simple method is to use a grid (figure 54:1). The squared paper on which these drawings have been made, make it easy to locate the points and mark off the scale.

Draw a grid of squares directly on the picture (or use tracing paper if you do not want to mark the picture). If the picture is very detailed, divide the grid into smaller units. Prepare a second grid on your drawing paper, which is larger or smaller than the grid on the original picture. Use a larger grid if you wish to enlarge and smaller one if you wish to reduce (figure 54:2).

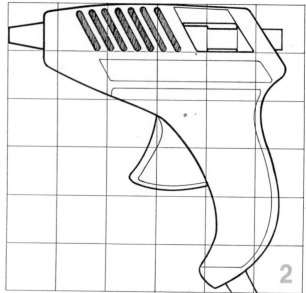

Figure 54

The Plan View

On page 4 you were asked to describe your route home from school using words or drawings. The simplest method of showing this information is to use a plan or map (figure 55:1). A plan is a view of an object or area as seen from above. Sometimes this is called a bird's-eye or aerial view, especially if the plan shows a room or street.

A plan can also be used to show the layout of smaller details. For example, figure 55:2 shows the position of keys on a 'credit card' calculator.

Figure 55:3 is a plan of a kitchen. Can you recognise the cooker and the sink on this plan? The dotted line represents the movements of a person working in the kitchen. Thicker lines have been used to show the main structures i.e. the walls. A thinner line is used to show the position of windows, doors cupboards etc. Plans show information about area, positions and measurements. It is important for a plan to be clear. The guidelines below will help.

- Measurements must be accurate.
- A scale should be indicated on the drawing.
- Decide what is important and should be shown on the plan. Leave out unnecessary information.
- Keep the plan as simple as possble.
- Colour coding sometimes helps to avoid confusion. For example, on Ordnance Survey maps, rivers are shown in blue while public footpaths are shown as red dotted lines.
- Supply a key where necessary to explain any symbols or signs you have used.

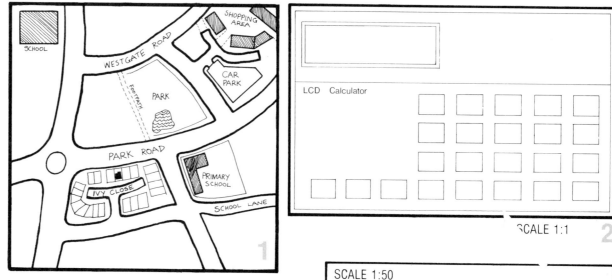

Figure 55

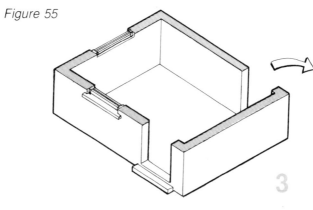

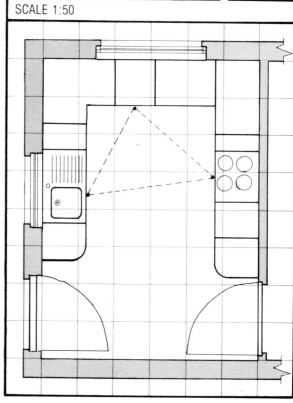

Scale

The plan drawing in figure 55:2 is the exact size of the actual calculator. The drawing of the kitchen however, is obviously much smaller than a real kitchen. If an object cannot be drawn full size, it is *scaled down* to fit onto the paper. The kitchen has been drawn to a scale of 1:50. This means that every milimetre of the plan is equal to 50 millimetres of real size. As the calculator is actual size, its scale is 1:1.

Graphs and Charts 1

The research into a design problem will involve collecting information. There are a number of ways to present statistics (numbers and amounts), so that they can be easily compared and understood. The three main types of charts for showing this information are:

(i) *graphs*,
(ii) *bar charts*, and
(iii) *pie charts*.

Although it is important to show the information accurately, you can make the presentation more interesting by using and developing some of the ideas on these pages.

Graphs

A graph is often used to show how something varies over a period of time. For example, a graph can be used to plot the changes in energy consumption in your home from month to month (figure 56:1).

■ All graphs must have clearly labelled horizontal and vertical scales.
■ Use squared graph paper or draw feint lines to form a grid. This will make it easier to plot each point.
■ If you have more than one line to plot on the same graph e.g. gas and electricity, each line must be clearly coded. (See figure 56:2.) You could use different colours or different types of line.

Bar charts

A bar chart is a simple method of comparing amounts. These amounts can be shown with vertical or horizontal blocks. The height of each block shows a quantity. If horizontal and vertical scales are not used, the block can be labelled with figures. The example in figure 56:3 shows in two ways, the number of pupils studying each subject in the 4th year of a school. What do you think figure 56:4 might show?

Figure 56

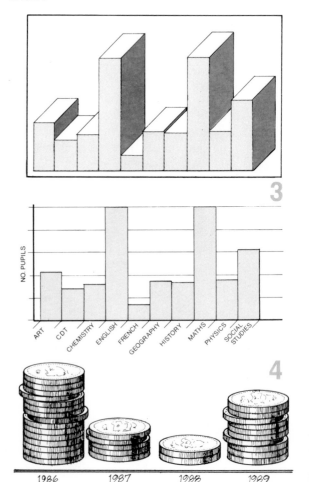

Pie charts

This type of diagram is usually circular, and can be divided into slices rather like a pie. Each slice or portion represents a statistic. This type of chart is good for showing how a total quantity is divided up into parts.

The circle represents 100% — the whole (figure 57:1). Portions are percentages of this. For example, figure 57:4 shows the results of a survey to find how many pupils in a class owned a computer. The number of computer owners was 14 out of a total class of 30. We know that this is nearly half of the class, so the pie chart will be divided approximately in half.

To show this *accurately* on the pie chart, we must make a simple calculation. The circle of the pie chart is made up of 360°. Since in this example, the circle represents the total class of 30, then the portion of circle for 1 pupil will be equal to 12° (360 ÷ 30 = 12). (See figure 57:2.) Fourteen pupils will be equal to 168° (14 × 12 = 168). (See figure 57:3.)

If the quantities you wish to show are percentages, then you can do a similar sum to above, but use 100 (100%) as the total. The percentage scale calculator in figure 57:5 will help you mark out accurately without calculation. It can be traced or used with thin drawing paper.

Always try to present pie charts in an interesting way. (See the examples in figure 57:6.)

Figure 57

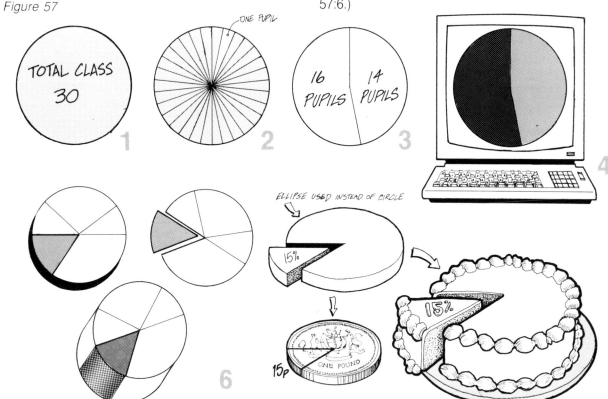

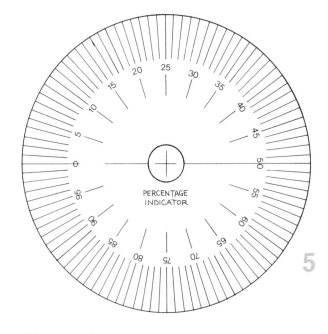

Pictographs

Simple pictures or symbols can be used to show the subject of a chart. These are called pictographs. What is the subject of the chart in figure 57:7?

With this type of chart you must give a key. This should show the quantity that is represented by each symbol.

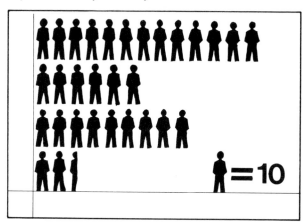

Sequence Diagrams

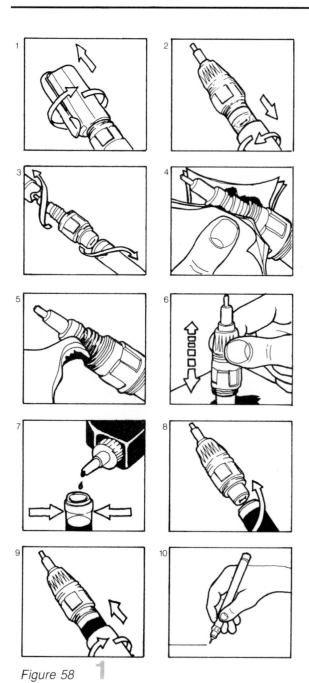

Figure 58 **1**

Sequence diagrams are a way of showing the order in which things happen. You will often find them used in instruction manuals, cookery books, leaflets supplied with model kits, and dress-making patterns.

The diagram in figure 58:1 illustrates a sequence of actions. What is described in this sequence? Each picture clearly shows how to perform the task. This type of diagram can be used to show any sequence of events or operations. It is easier to understand a diagram than a lengthy written explanation. However, a sequence diagram can be made using simple keywords to explain the process (figure 58:2).

Which of these two diagrams do you think gives the clearest explanation?

To make a sequence diagram you must decide on:

- how much information to give,
- how many steps or stages are involved,
- the correct order of these stages.

Sequence diagrams must be well organised so that they are easy to follow. Words or pictures must be simple, clear and easy to understand. Frames can be used to contain the information with arrows leading the eye from frame to frame. Use a sequence diagram to describe how to do one of the following:

(i)   make a permanent joint between two pieces of wood,

(ii) make a temporary joint between pieces of sheet metal,

(iii) correctly sew a button to a piece of cloth.

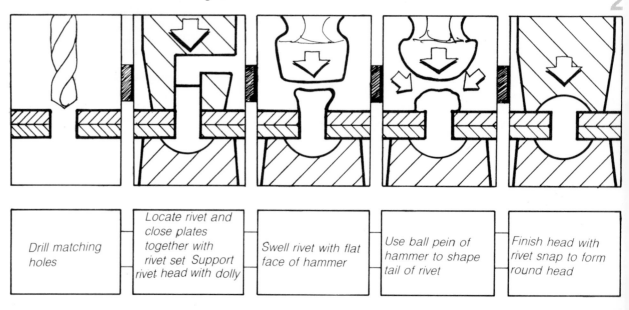

| Drill matching holes | Locate rivet and close plates together with rivet set Support rivet head with dolly | Swell rivet with flat face of hammer | Use ball pein of hammer to shape tail of rivet | Finish head with rivet snap to form round head |

Drawing People 1

Most of the things we design are intended to be used by human beings; yet very few design drawings contain sketches of the human figure. People often assume that it is very difficult to draw figures, and try to avoid putting them into their drawings. However, it is easier to produce a reasonable human figure if the drawing is attempted in easy stages.

As most objects we design will be made for human use, it is important to show how the object is to be used or operated. For example, if designing a desk, it is necessary to show how a person would sit at the desk, what positions they would adopt when working, and if they look comfortable. The study of people in relation to their surroundings is known as *ergonomics*. An *Ergonome* is a moveable *template* of the human form (figure 59:1) and is used by designers to help them estimate body positions.

You will need to know the basic proportions of the human body before you can draw a figure in various positions. Make your own ergonome using the drawing in figure 59:1 as a pattern. You can use thin card or plastic sheet and paper fasteners for the joints. Remember to draw and cut out the different parts separately, and then join them together.

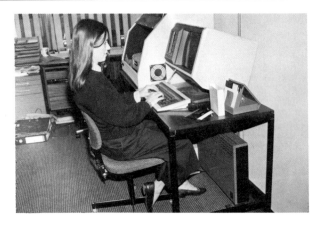

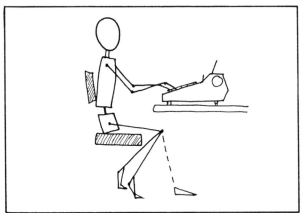

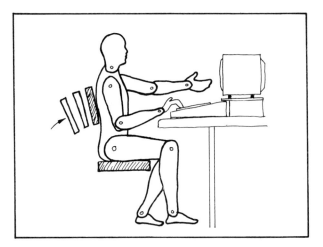

Figure 59

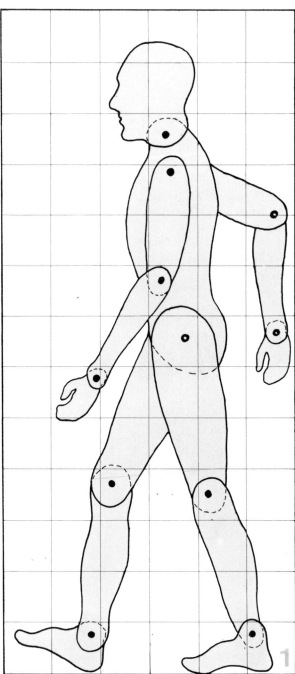

Drawing People 2

A quick way of drawing a person is to sketch a simple framework. Remember the proportions of the figure and construct the skeleton of the drawing using boxes and lines (figure 60:2). The details and bulk can be added to the drawing at a later stage.

It is important to keep detail on the figure to a minimum. The outline is all that is required for most design drawings. Unnecessary detail will only draw attention away from the object you are designing and will make the drawing appear cluttered.

The human figure can be divided into seven equal parts (figure 60:1). The head is approximately one seventh of the total height. This information provides us with a convenient way of measuring the whole body which is roughly seven heads high in total. The top of the legs are about three heads above ground level. The shoulders are three heads above this.

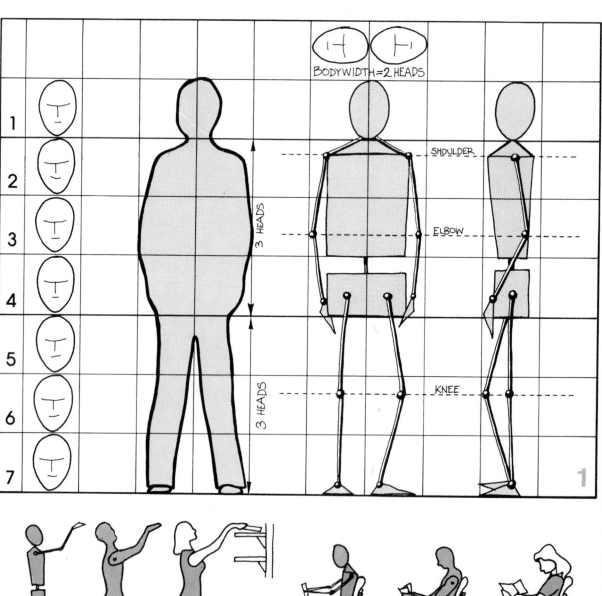

Figure 60

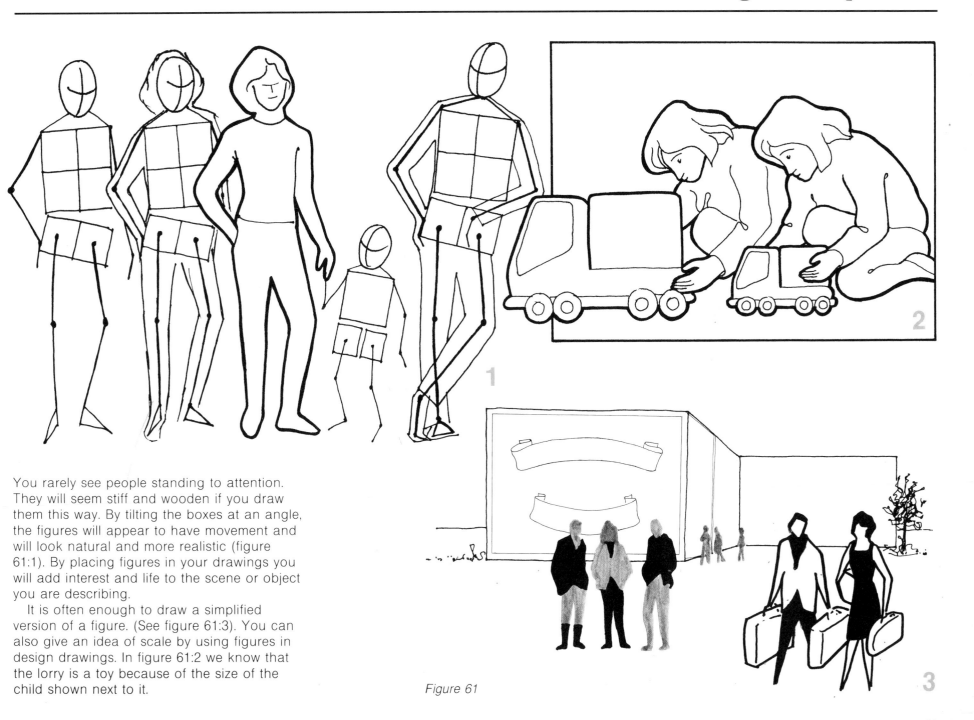

You rarely see people standing to attention. They will seem stiff and wooden if you draw them this way. By tilting the boxes at an angle, the figures will appear to have movement and will look natural and more realistic (figure 61:1). By placing figures in your drawings you will add interest and life to the scene or object you are describing.

It is often enough to draw a simplified version of a figure. (See figure 61:3). You can also give an idea of scale by using figures in design drawings. In figure 61:2 we know that the lorry is a toy because of the size of the child shown next to it.

Figure 61

Computer-Aided Design 1

A computer is the latest tool available to us when solving design problems. It can test a design solution, pin-point faults and make detailed drawings from which we can produce a final design. However, a computer needs to be given very precise instructions in order for it to do any of these things. These instructions are called a *program*.

A computer can only do what a program or programmer tells it to do. Simple programs are typed into the computer on a keyboard. More complicated programs, written by experienced programmers, can be fed into the computer from an audio-cassette or disk.

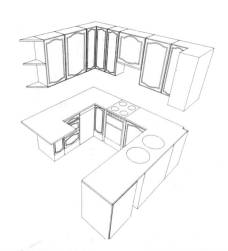

The computer as a design tool

Many different factors need to be considered when solving design problems. For example, the design of a motor car is a very long and complicated task. How will the materials used in its design be affected by weather conditions, stress or vibration? Is the design aerodynamic? Have ergonomic factors been considered?

In this type of design work where many people may be working on one design project, the computer can store all the information required about each aspect of the design.

If a computer is supplied with the correct data (information) it can display a model of this data on the screen of a video display unit (VDU). This will help the designer to answer

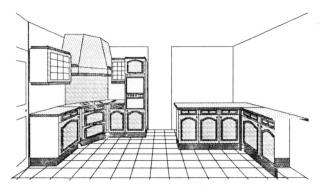

some of his/her questions. Once the design data is in the computer's memory it can be stored, ready to be called up instantly whenever required. The computer can be programmed so that the design can be changed in some way, for instance its shape may be altered or parts added or removed. The design can be rotated and looked at from all angles. At any stage in this process, the computer can be asked to produce a print-out of the image on the screen.

Drawing with a computer

Drawing with a computer usually involves directing a cursor or marker on the screen of the VDU. This moving cursor produces the lines. There are a number of ways that this can be done:

■ Commands can be typed in or cursor control keys can be used on the *keyboard*.
■ A *light-pen* can be pointed at the display on the screen.
■ A *digitising tablet* can be used with a stylus.
■ A *joystick* or *tracker ball* can direct the cursor on the screen.
■ A *mouse* moving over a flat surface or drawing will convey its position to the computer.

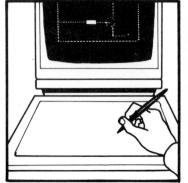

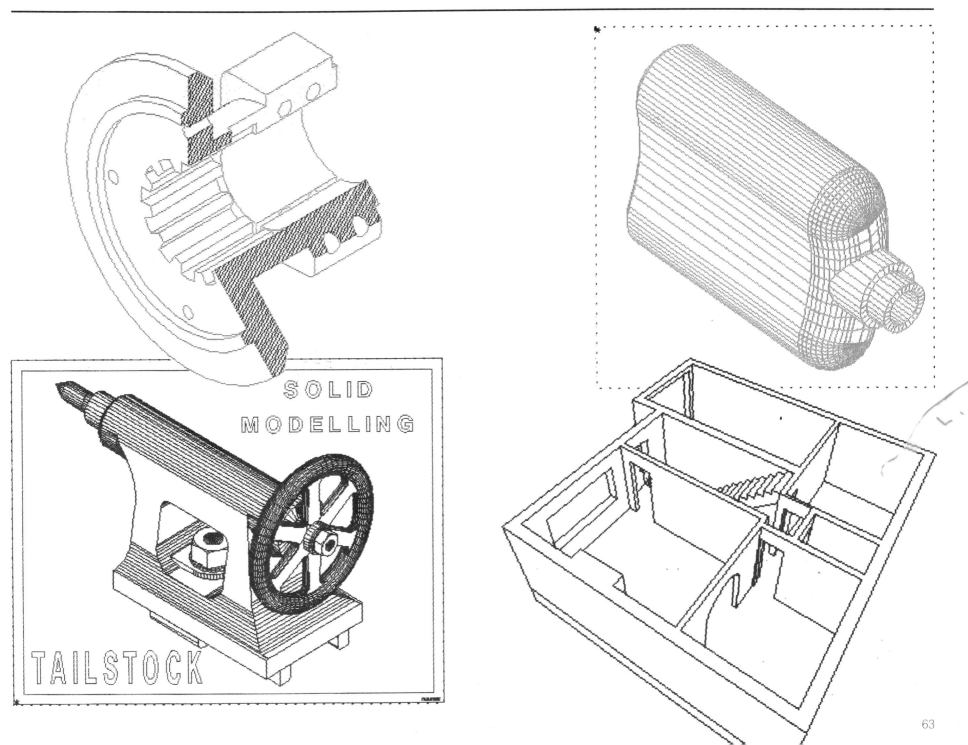

SOLID

MODELLING

TAILSTOCK

Assignments 4

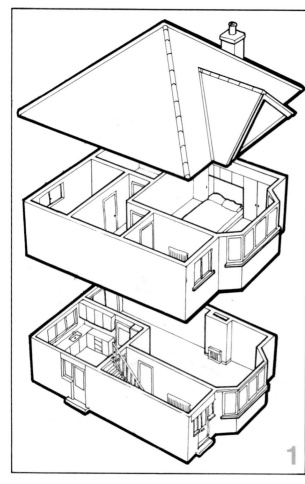

Figure 64

1 The illustration in figure 64:1 shows an exploded view of a house. It clearly shows the layout, and relationship of rooms to each other.

Choose a building that you are familiar with, and construct an exploded view of it, using a method of pictorial projection of your own choice. (See pages 17 and 52.)

2 Using a sequence of 6 line drawings, describe how to perform one of the tasks from the list below:
(i)   making a sandwich,
(ii) making a cross-halving joint,
(iii) hanging a length of wallpaper,
(iv) making a clay thumbpot. (See page 58.)

3 Draw the outline of a person performing *two* of the following activities:
(i)   sitting in a chair reading,
(ii) reaching up to a high shelf,
(iii) removing something from an oven,
(iv) carrying a heavy object,
(v)   using an electric drill. (See pages 59 and 60.)

4 Design a small landscaped area for a town centre. It can contain such things as benches, a fountain, and planted area. Place at least three simplified figures in your drawing to show the scale of your design. (See pge 61.)

5 Carefully study one of the objects from the list below, and produce an accurate, dimensioned, orthographic projection of it showing plan, end and front views.
(i)   a hairdryer
(ii) a camera
(iii) a cassette recorder
(v)   an electric kettle

6 Conduct a survey of how the people in your class travel to school/college. Record and present your findings as either:
        (i)   a pie chart,
        (ii) a pictogram,
or (iii) a bar chart.
Present your chart in a form which is suitable for the subject i.e. transport. (See pages 56 and 57.)

7 Draw a scale plan of your kitchen, including furniture and fittings. Draw on the plan, using lines, the movement of the person preparing the main meal of the day. Your plan will show the most used areas of the kitchen. Suggest improvements that would reduce the distance covered during the preparation of a meal.

8 Using exploded views, illustrate various methods of attaching wheels to wooden toys. These toys are to be used by young children, so you will need to show safety features where appropriate.

Colour

A very important part of design is the use of colour. Colour will possibly be the biggest influence on our choice when we buy something — whether it is a can of soft drink or a new car. Colour can help transform a plain, dull object to a lively, exciting one. Have you ever considered why we use brightly coloured wrapping paper for gifts? Why are childrens' toys often made in vivid colours? Can you think of any other examples where colour is used to make something seem more attractive?

All colours affect our moods and feelings. Blue for example, can make us feel chilled or give a feeling of loneliness. Blues and greens used in the design of a toothpaste tube will help to create the impression of cool 'mintyness'. An orange-red colour, however, can make us feel warm and comfortable. A strong red can cause irritation and restlesness.

In order to shock or gain our attention, designers use strong, outstanding colours, such as red, yellow and blue. It is these three colours — known as the *primary colours* — that our eye is drawn to most readily.

Colour in design drawings

Knowledge of how colours affect us will help when we begin to use colour in design drawing. Any colours used in a drawing will focus attention on the page. However, you must take care that the colour does not overpower the actual object you have drawn (i.e. the viewer may be drawn to the strong colour but not the design idea).

Remember that you are using drawing to communicate your ideas. Colour must only be used as a method of improving this communication. The *careful* use of colour will help you achieve this. Colour can be used not only to make the drawing more attractive, but also to do a particular job. It is used to:

■ show the suggested colour scheme of a design,
■ help show the materials of which an object is made, e.g. oak or mahogany, aluminium or brass,
■ outline a sketch on a design sheet,
■ tint the background to a drawing to help make it stand out,
■ colour code different areas, e.g. wiring on a diagram or circuit,
■ show different components, e.g. parts of an engine,
■ make an object look solid or 3D by using different tones,
■ highlight the most important part of the drawing.

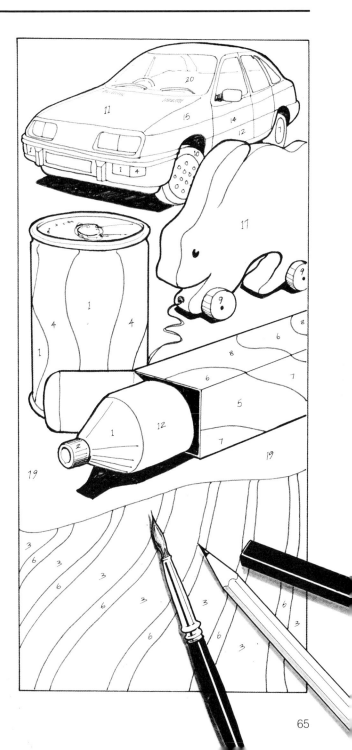

The Language of Colour

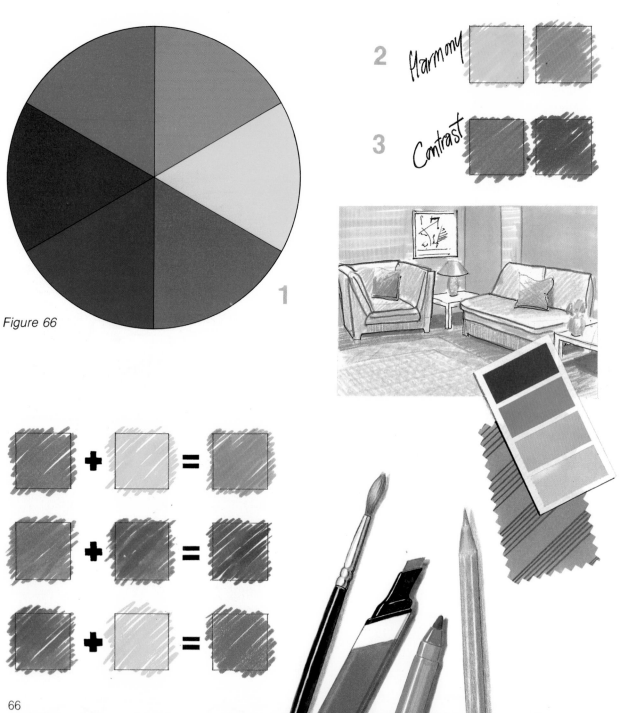

Figure 66

Harmony

3 Contrast

Many people confuse the words we use to describe colour. Here are some commonly used words, with their meanings. Learn to use them correctly.

■ *The colour wheel* is a diagram which shows how colours relate to each other. It is usually made up of a circle divided into six segments, each containing a different colour — red, orange, yellow, green, blue and violet (figure 66;1), The wheel is based on the theory that all colours can be made from the three primary colours.

■ Colours that are next (or close) to each other on the colour wheel will *harmonise* (look comfortable or agreeable together). (Figure 66:2.)

■ Colours that *contrast* with each other (clash) are called *complimentary colours*. These are opposite each other on the colour wheel (figure 66:3).

■ *primary* colours are red, yellow and blue. They cannot be mixed from any other colours.

■ The *secondary* colours are violet, green and orange. These are made by mixing two primary colours together, e.g.

   red + yellow   = orange
   red + blue   = violet
   blue + yellow = green

■ *tone* is used to describe lighter or darker versions of the same colour. A lighter tone of a colour is called a *tint* i.e. a colour mixed with white. A darker tone of a colour is called a *shade* i.e. a colour mixed with black.

Cut out samples of colours from magazines and find:
(i)   two colours that *contrast*,
(ii) a group of colours that *harmonize*,
(iii) three *tones* of one colour.

Do not underate the value of pencil crayons for colouring design drawings. They are excellent for adding 'instant' colour to design sketches. They are quick to use, easy to control, inexpensive and involve no mess. When used more carefully, pencil crayons are also ideal for producing more finished presentation drawings. The illustrations on this page and page 68 show a range of techniques that will help you use your pencil crayons more effectively.

Just one blue crayon has been used to produce all of the different tones of blue in figure 67:1. The very light blues resulted from very gentle use of the pencil crayon. The darker blues were made by pressing slighty harder on the crayon and by working over the same area several times.

New shades and colours can be made by mixing the crayons. Even if you only have the primary colours (red, yellow, and blue) you can create all of the colours in figure 67:2. This can be achieved through careful *overlaying* of the different crayons. As a general rule start with the lighter colours first.

The drawings for the design of a brush, above, show several different uses of a *pencil crayon*.

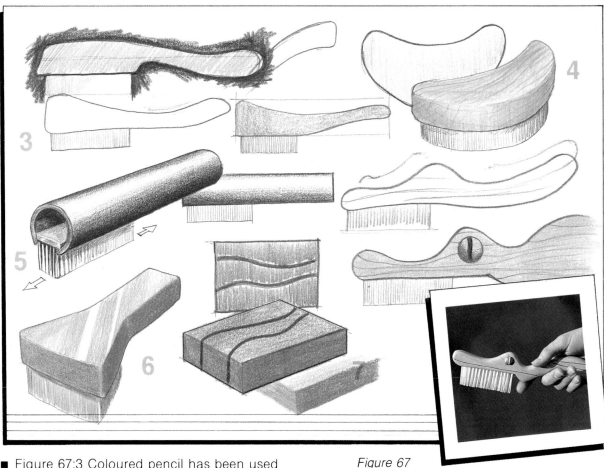

Figure 67

■ Figure 67:3 Coloured pencil has been used to outline an idea and to emphasize the shape
■ Figure 67:4 Yellow, orange and brown crayons have been used together to show the colour and texture of the wooden handle.
■ Figure 67:5 Varying the tone can give the effect of a curved surface.
■ Figure 67:6 Just *one* crayon has been used to make the three different tones which make the brush look more solid.
■ Figure 67:7 *Two* crayons, (a light green and a dark green) have been used to create a three-dimensional effect.

Use one coloured crayon to produce as many different *tones* of that colour as possible. (See figure 67:1.)

Using only red, yellow and blue pencil crayons make as many different *colours* as you can. (See figure 67:2.)

Pencil Crayons 2

The following hints will help you produce better results with your pencil crayons:

■ Keep a sharp point on your crayon.
■ When colouring, do not keep changing direction with the pencil crayon.
■ Colour up to the exact edges of shapes.
■ To obtain flat, even colour, keep the same pressure on the crayon.
■ Only use the pencil crayon to perform a specific job, e.g. to help show the material an object is made from.
■ Do not overcolour — a little colour looks more effective than too much.
■ Colours produced by mixing crayons look more interesting.

There are many different types of pencil crayon available, and their 'softness' varies according to the range and make. For example, some coloured pencils have thinner, slightly harder leads, which are good for fine detail drawing.

Figure 68

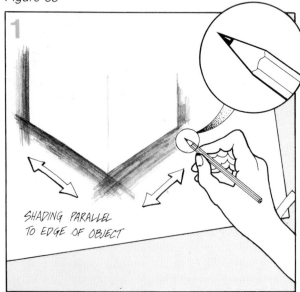

SHADING PARALLEL TO EDGE OF OBJECT

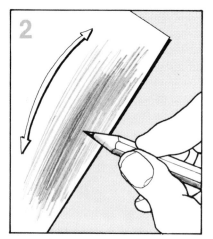

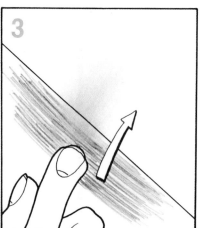

Soft-edged effects

The drawings above show a different way of using pencil crayons. The crayon is smudged onto the paper to create a soft-edged area of colour.

■ Apply plenty of crayon close to the folded edge of some scrap paper.
■ Place this right up to the outline of the object that you have drawn in lightly (figure 68:2).
■ Use your thumb or finger to smudge the colour evenly towards the centre of the object (figure 68:3).

This should produce an area of subtle colour. This is a good technique for showing any material with a smooth surface, e.g. glass, plastics, metal. (See figure 68:4).

Water-soluble crayons

Certain types of pencil crayons can be used to create similar effects to water colour paints. These are known as water-soluble crayons. They can be used with water to produce washes of colour. The pencil crayon is used as normal, and then 'washed' over the paper with a clean brush and water (figure 68:5).

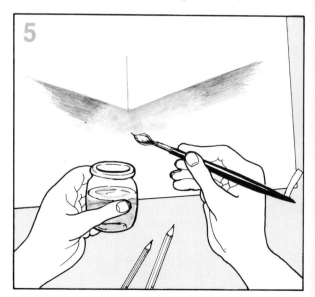

One of the newest additions to the range of graphics materials is the marker pen. They have become very popular because of their free-flowing, quick-drying colours. Marker pens offer the advantages of paints, with their strong colours and ability to cover wide areas yet are instant and non-messy! The makers of these pens are continually producing new colours and types of marker which are designed to do certain jobs e.g. floppy disk pens, metallic colour pens and fluorescent colours for highlighting.

Types of markers

Two particular types of markers are favoured by designers. These are the *fine-line marker* and the broader nibbed *studio marker*. On the whole, these pens are more expensive than the ordinary felt-tip pens but they are of a much higher quality. Ordinary felt pens can be obtained in large sets at low prices. However, they tend to dry up quickly and the felt or fibre-tip soon loses its shape. Also, the colours are often different to those shown on the pen.

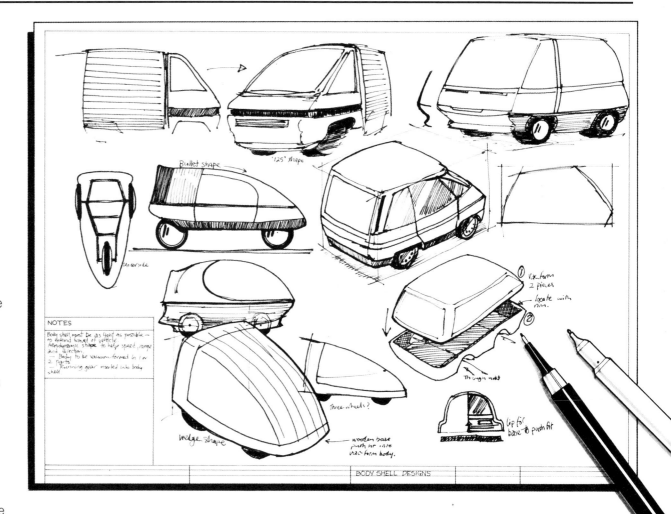

Paper

Markers can be divided into two types — those which contain *spirit-based inks* and those with *water-based inks*.

■ Spirit-based markers tend to 'bleed' (soak) through normal papers and will stain anything beneath the paper such as the desk or other drawings! Special marker paper can be bought which has a coating on the back to stop the ink from soaking through. Alternatively, high grade tracing paper can be used.

■ Markers which contain water-based inks, do not tend to bleed through the paper. These inks are usually transparent and colours can be applied over one another to build up a limited range of tones and colours.

If you are not sure whether the marker you are using is going to bleed through the paper or not, you should place some scrap paper beneath your drawing.

Fine-line markers

Many of the design drawings, sketches and notes in this book have been made with a fine line marker. These pens are popular because they can be used like pencils for quick sketches yet also give a thin bold line similar to a technical pen.

The figure shows a typical design sheet produced with a fine line marker.

Markers 2

Most people will be familiar with the type of marker used on this page. These are the brightly coloured *felt* or *fibre-tipped* pens which are popular for colouring-in. However, the use of such bright colours is often unsuitable for design sketches as they tend to look harsh or garish, and can be overpowering. Only the more subtle shades, such as grey or brown, can be effective for outlining a design idea or picking out details.

The examples on this page show that these strong colours can be useful when illustrating objects with brightly coloured finishes, such as toys and packaging.

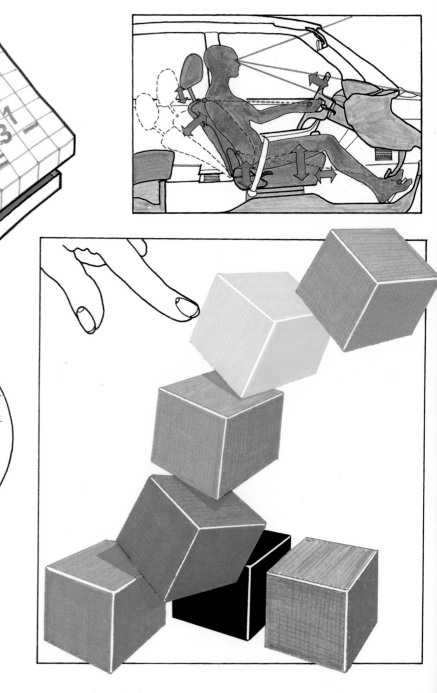

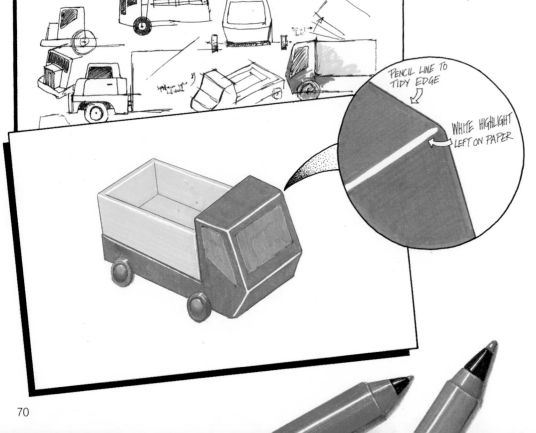

PENCIL LINE TO TIDY EDGE

WHITE HIGHLIGHT LEFT ON PAPER

This drawing (figure 71:4) has been built up in simple stages using *studio markers*. You can see that the drawing really starts to sharpen-up when the details have been put in. It is the highlights, shadows and reflections, added using crayon and paint, that bring the drawing to life.

■ Draw the object in lightly with a pencil. Decide where highlights and shade will fall (figure 71:1).

■ Using parallel strokes, fill in the shape with the main colour. Do not worry about going over the edges, as the final drawing will be cut out. Leave a white area if you wish to create a dramatic highlight (figure 71:2).

■ When dry, work over with the same marker to make darker areas (the areas in shade). This is called *overcoating* (figure 71:3).

■ Add colours for switches etc.

■ Highlights on the edges of the object can be drawn in with a white crayon or paint. Shadow details are picked out with a black crayon or fine-line marker

■ Cut out the finished drawing. Stick it carefully on to a suitable background (figure 71:4).

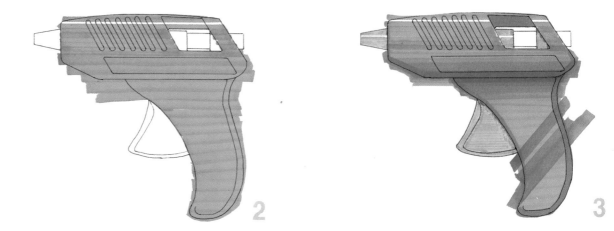

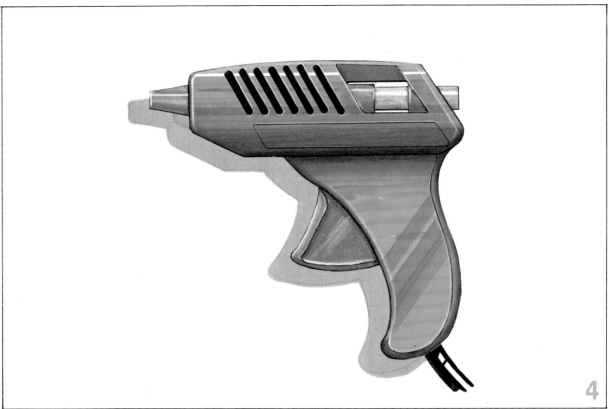

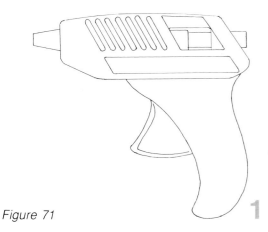

Figure 71

Studio Markers 2

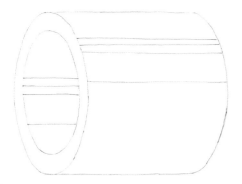

The biggest advantage that studio markers have over ordinary felt-tips, is that they are available in many different colours. For example, at least fifteen different shades of grey marker are available. This means that it is possible to choose exactly the colour needed for a particular job. You can also recreate the effect of light and shade on an object by using lighter and darker tones of one colour. With this in mind, it may be wise to buy one colour in two or three related tones (e.g. dark blue, mid-blue, light blue) rather than a range of unrelated colours like blue, red and green.

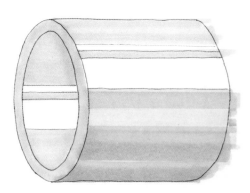

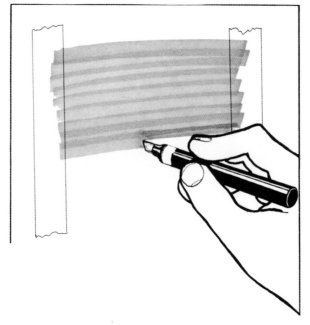

Basic techniques

It is important to remember that studio markers are not used in the same way as pencils or crayons. With practice you will gain the confidence needed to work boldly and achieve the best results with the marker.

■ Draw the outline in pencil first. Do *not* attempt to draw with a studio marker. Decide what type of finish the object will have e.g. glossy or matt. Plan where highlights and areas of light and shade will occur.
■ Start with the lightest tone of marker and work up to the darkest tones. Darker tones can be made by overcoating a second or third layer of marker, or by using a darker shade of pen.
■ Do not worry about working over edges. The outline can be masked off with tape, or the finished drawing can be cut out and pasted onto a background.
■ To obtain even colour, keep the marker moving at the same speed and pressure across the paper. Do not overlap strokes of the marker (unless darkening the tone) or a streaky effect will result.
■ You can use the direction of marker strokes to help show the form of the object.

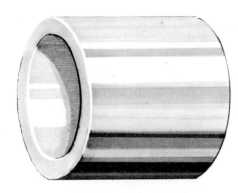

The name 'pastel' comes from the word 'paste'. Pastels are made from powdered colour, mixed into a paste with gum or resin. This paste is then formed into a stick and allowed to dry. About 600 colours and tints are available, but you will only need a few of these for the types of design drawings shown on these pages. Pastels can be used in their stick form for sketching, especially on coloured paper. However, designers have developed an effective technique that makes use of the powdery quality of the pastel stick. Rather than drawing with the pastel onto the paper in the usual way, it is rubbed on, using tissue or cotton wool. (See figure 73:2) This produces a flat, smooth area of colour with soft edges. You will find that it is difficult to obtain a sharp outline using this method. A solution to this problem is to use a *mask* (made of paper, card or masking tape,). The mask is used to keep the pastel within an area you wish to colour. If you use tape, make sure that is does not rip the paper when you remove it. Highlights and reflections on surfaces can be made by removing some of the pastel with an eraser. (See figure 73:3.)

Fixatives

To stop your finished pastel drawing from smudging you can spray it with a fixative.

Fixatives act as a seal and will 'fix' your powdered pastel to the paper. They are available in aerosol cans, or can be sprayed from a bottle with a spray diffuser. Unfortunately some fixatives may dull the pastel. Therefore, it is important to give a light coat of spray, holding the can at a distance of about 30 centimetres. Alternatively, the drawing may be sprayed from the back and the fixative allowed to soak through.

N.B. Avoid breathing in the fixative spray as it may be harmful.

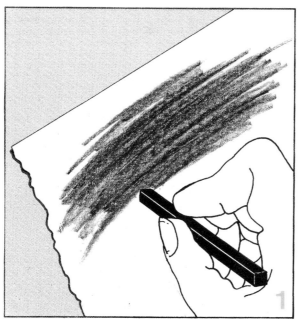

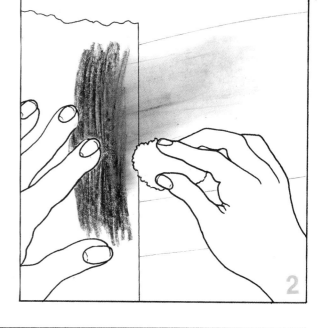

Figure 73

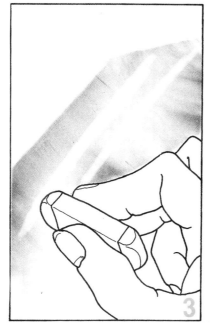

Pastels 2

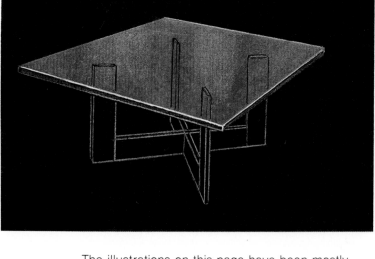

The illustrations on this page have been mostly made with pastels. Can you see that some of the colours have been created by mixing different pastels together? Note that the details have been added with different media, i.e. pencil crayons, markers etc. A striking effect has been achieved by using the pastel on a dark background.

Telephone: red pastel brushed over masked areas; red marker for shade areas highlights rubbed out with putty rubber or painted in with white gouache, cut-out and pasted onto blue pastel background

Table: white pastel and pencil crayon on black Ingres paper

Vehicle: Wheels and shadow detail blocked in with black marker; pastel brushed across vehicle; highlights rubbed out with putty rubber; detail lines added with fine line marker; cut out and mounted onto prepared background
Background: pastel smudged with airbrush cleaning medium; rectangle masked with tape

Painting with water-based paints is the traditional method of colouring design drawings. People sometimes avoid using paints on design work, because they find them difficult to control. However, if paints are used carefully and in an organised way, very effective results can be achieved.

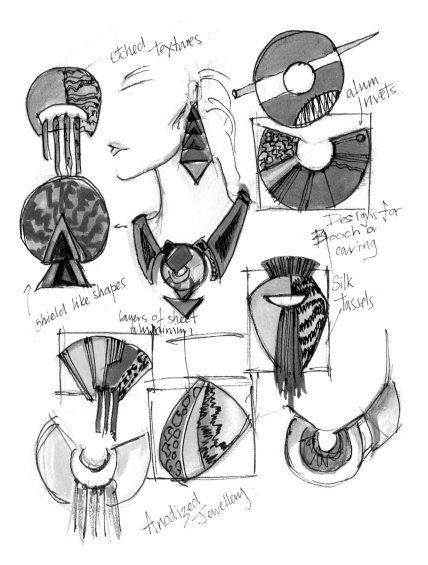

etched textures

alum rivets

shield like shapes

Designs for Booch or earring

Silk tassels

layers of sheet aluminium

Anodized Jewellery

Water-soluble Paints 2

There are many different types of paint that can be mixed with water. All of these paints will have the effect of buckling the paper, especially when mixed with a lot of water. To avoid this you can stretch the paper. (See figure 76.1.) Alternatively, thicker cartridge paper, board, or special watercolour paper can be used.

Stretching paper

So that paper does not buckle and pull out of shape when soaked with paint, it should be stretched onto a board. This may be done before or after the pencil sketching stage.

■ Use a sponge to thoroughly soak the paper with clean water.
■ Allow extra water to drain off.
■ Lay the paper flat on a board.
■ Fix the paper to the board with two inch gummed tape. Tape the opposite ends first. (See figure 76.1.)
■ Allow to dry naturally.

Water colour

Water colours are available in blocks, tubes or as a liquid in bottles. Of these, the dried blocks of paint are probably the least expensive, and last the longest. Water colour is usually applied in transparent (see-through) washes over pen or pencil drawings, allowing the lines to show through. A small amount of paint is diluted with a large amount of water to make a colour wash. It is important to remember when using water colour, that you are using transparent colours. Colours are lightened by thinning them with water and not by adding white paint to them. This should mean that the lightest tone in your picture is the white of the paper. Darker tones, such as shadows, can be made in three ways:

(i)   by adding blue or black to the colour wash,
(ii) by adding more colour to the wash,
(iii) by allowing the first wash to dry and applying a second or third coat on top.

Flat water colour wash

This technique is used for backgrounds.
■ Damp your paper with a large brush or sponge (figure 76:2).
■ Mix enough paint to cover the whole paper.
■ Tilt the board towards you at an angle so the wash will flow easily.
■ Load the brush with plenty of paint and draw a stroke along the top of the paper (figure 76:3).
■ Continue with broad, horizontal strokes until you have covered the whole area. Excess paint will run down to the bottom of your paper. This can be mopped up with a dry brush (figure 76:4).

Figure 76

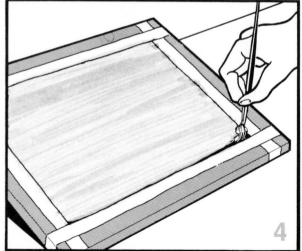

o Apply weak colour wash to all surfaces

o Second wash — Top surface NOT given second wash

o Third Wash — Surface facing away from light

Figure 77 **1**

Water colour washes can also be used to make objects look more solid (figure 77:1). Imagine that the object is divided into three separate areas: light, medium and dark.

- Draw the object lightly in pencil.
- Apply a weak colour wash to the whole of the object and allow it to dry.
- Colour-wash all surfaces of the object for a second time, except the surface which directly faces the light. Allow it to dry.
- Give a third colour wash to the surface facing away from the light source. This should now have the darkest tone.

Gouache and poster colour

Gouache and poster colour are basically water colours with white added. This completely changes the character of the paint, and a different technique of working is needed. This addition of white takes away the transparency of the paint. It becomes *opaque* (not see-through). You will find that the paper or your drawing is no longer visible through the paint. These opaque paints are most useful for:
(i)   painting areas of flat, even colour,
(ii) working over colour backgrounds,
(iii) laying lighter tones of colour over dark areas such as highlights,
(iv) obtaining strong, vivid colours.
Colours come in tubes or jars ranging from inexpensive powder paints to high quality designers gouache.

o Surface pattern added with gouache

o TABLE LAMP o

Airbrush 1

Airbrush illustration of a car for the physically disabled. GKN Sankey (1978).

Figure 78

1

Airbrush

2

An airbrush is not a magic drawing tool! You will need time and practise to become skilled in its use. However, of all the drawing techniques shown in this book, airbrush work produces the most professional and realistic results.

How an airbrush works

Basically, all airbrushes work by mixing air under pressure with paint to produce a fine spray. This is called *atomising*. There are two main types of airbrush.

A *single-action airbrush*, is the simplest type, having only one control which determines the amount of air that is released with the paint. The only way to alter the area of spray is to move the airbrush away from, or nearer to, the paper. Single-action airbrushes are quite easy to operate, but are only really suitable for flat areas or backgrounds.

Double-action airbrushes have an added control over the flow of paint (as well as the air). The control lever operates both air and paint. A downward pressure controls the air supply and a backward movement releases the paint into the jet of air (figure 78:1). By careful control it is possible to produce broad areas of tone, or thin lines for detail work (figure 78:2).

Air supply

All airbrushes need a supply of *compressed air* (air under pressure) to spray the paint. Air can be obtained in aerosol cans, from an electric compressor, or even from a car inner tube which has been fitted with an adaptor to accept the air hose.

Colours for the airbrush

It is important that the colours used in an airbrush are of the correct consistency. They should be thin enough to pass through the airbrush without clogging it up. As a general guide, the liquid should be the consistency of milk and be easily washed away with water.

Gouache or water colours are most often used in airbrushes since the particles of colour in them are finely ground. Liquid water colours can be bought in jars, which are ready mixed to the correct consistency.

Poster colour is not suitable as it contains large particles which can clog the airbrush.

Airbrushes are expensive items. It is essential that they are cleaned and looked after very carefully. If an airbrush is neglected and paint is allowed to dry inside, it will clog and can completely ruin the airbrush. It is important to follow the manufacturers cleaning instructions after every use.

Do *not* attempt to take an airbrush apart!

First Steps

For spraying *flat tones*, use smooth, sweeping movements across the paper. Hold the airbrush about 10 cm away from the paper.

For spraying *lines*, move the airbrush closer to the paper. Reduce the amount of air and paint released by easing your finger off the lever. If your line is too 'spidery', you have allowed too much paint or air through.

Cube

Figure 79.1 shows how to produce a cube. The different tones have been achieved by removing sections 1, 2 and 3 of the mask, one after another. This results in a dense build up of colour in the areas most exposed to the spray.

Sphere

Only one mask is needed to airbrush a sphere An impression of volume must be built up using feehand sweeps of the airbrush. Cut a circular hole to form the mask and build-up the tones gradually as shown in figure 79:2. Notice where the highlight has been created on the sphere. Which direction is the light shining from?

Cylinder

Decide where the areas of highlight and darkest tone will be. It is these bands of light and dark which give the impression of a curved surface. Cut out a mask as in figure 79:3. Spray in the areas of tone along the cylinder using freehand parallel strokes of the airbrush.

You will need to spray over certain areas several times to build up the darkest tones. Replace and weight down the mask before you spray an even tone over the end of the cylinder (figure 79:4).

Drawings can be sharpened-up and details added with pencil crayons or paint.

Masking

The most important feature of any airbrush work will be the masks that are used. A mask is simply anything that stops the spray reaching the paper. This is the only way that the spread of the airbrush spray can be controlled, and a 'hard edge' obtained. A special low-tack masking film can be bought for this purpose, but paper, card or masking tape are adequate and less expensive substitutes.

■ When spraying a section which has been masked off, you must make sure that the mask is large enough to protect other areas of the drawing from overspray.
■ To prevent a paper or card mask from moving under the force of the spray, you can use coins to weight the mask down.
■ Begin spraying on the masked part of the drawing, and finish on the mask. This will help to avoid uneven spray on the drawing.

Figure 79

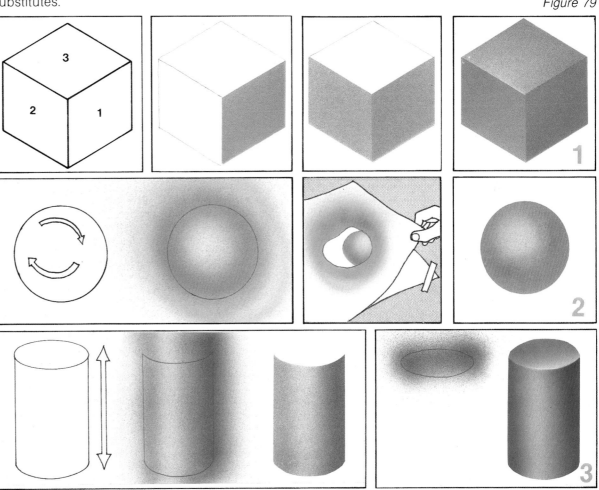

Assignments 5

1 Using poster colours or gouache, produce a brightly-coloured design for a paper or plastic carrier bag. Your carrier should be suitable for one of the following shops:
(i)   a greengrocers,
(ii) a wine merchant,
(iii) a DIY store,
(iv) a record shop.

2 Produce design sketches for protective clothing for either:
(i)   a hill walker,
(ii) a cyclist,
(iii) a foundry worker (a person working with hot metals).
Use water colour for your final presentation drawing. Use notes to describe your choice of material, fastenings etc.,

3 You are supplied with a small quartz clock movement. Design a novelty clock to be used in one of the following areas:
(i)   a play school,
(ii) a kitchen,
(iii) a travel agency.
Begin by using coloured papers. Experiment with different shape and colour arrangements. Present your final design as a full-scale colour mock-up.

4 A soft drinks company has produced a new tropical fruit cocktail drink. You are required to produce ideas for:
(a) the name of the drink,
(b) the colour scheme and designs for the carton.
Your colour scheme should reflect the exotic image of the product. (See pages 65, 66 and 70.)

5 Design a range of 'fun' jewellery to be made from unusual materials. For example: electrical cable, coloured nylon cords, feathers, washers, scraps of leather, sequins, rubber, PVC, or offcuts of acrylic. Record your ideas in colour, using pencil crayons.

6 Design a logo and colour scheme to be painted on the van drawn in figure 80:1, which would be suitable for one of the following businesses:
(i)   a painter and decorator,
(ii) a plumber,
(iii) a florist.
   Use the grid to draw an enlarged outline of the van onto your paper. (See page 54.)

Figure 80 1

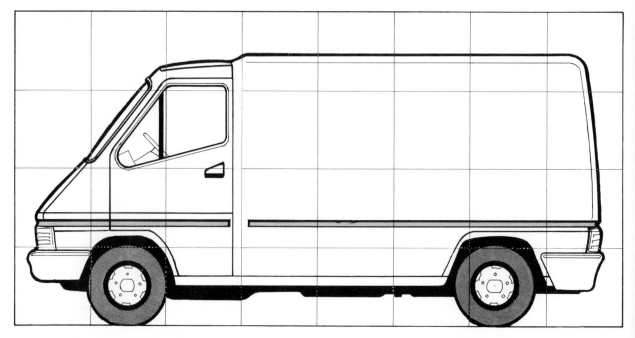

Coloured paper is an excellent base for drawing objects that are transparent or mainly one colour. The colour of the paper is used as the medium tone of the drawing. Light and shade is added with crayon, pastel or marker. Remember that the object does not need to be coloured in further. The paper itself provides the colour.

An effective presentation can be obtained quite simply if an orthographic drawing is already available (figure 81:1). Although the illustration gives a realistic impression, it is based on two flat views of the object. This can have a number of advantages.

(i) Views can be taken directly from an orthographic drawing by tracing or photocopying.
(ii) Where there are curved or circular details they can be drawn as 'true shapes', without having to construct ellipses etc.
(iii) A blueprint made from a tracing can be used as a coloured background.
(iv) The colour of the object can be suggested simply by the choice of the background paper.

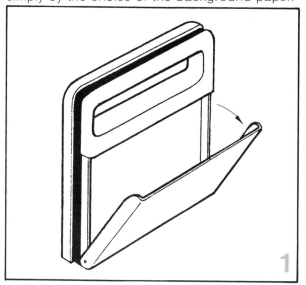

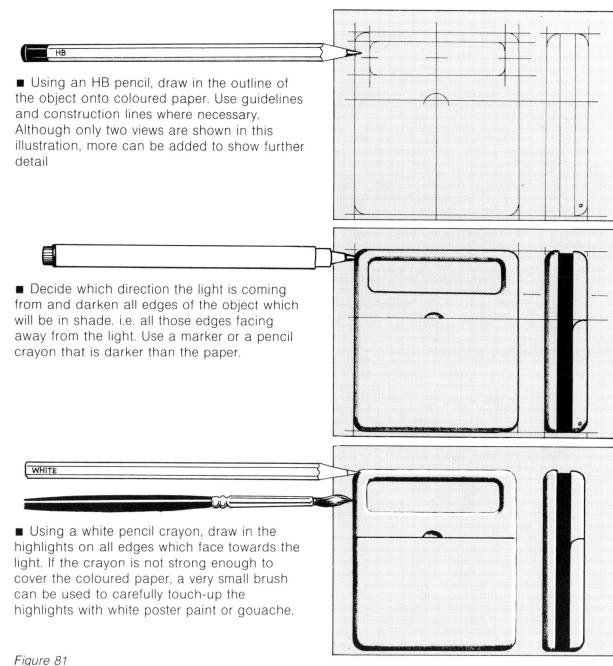

■ Using an HB pencil, draw in the outline of the object onto coloured paper. Use guidelines and construction lines where necessary. Although only two views are shown in this illustration, more can be added to show further detail

■ Decide which direction the light is coming from and darken all edges of the object which will be in shade. i.e. all those edges facing away from the light. Use a marker or a pencil crayon that is darker than the paper.

■ Using a white pencil crayon, draw in the highlights on all edges which face towards the light. If the crayon is not strong enough to cover the coloured paper, a very small brush can be used to carefully touch-up the highlights with white poster paint or gouache.

Figure 81

Coloured Paper 2

The drawings on this page show flat views of objects drawn on coloured paper. On one example the outline has been emphasised by colouring some of the background with a crayon.

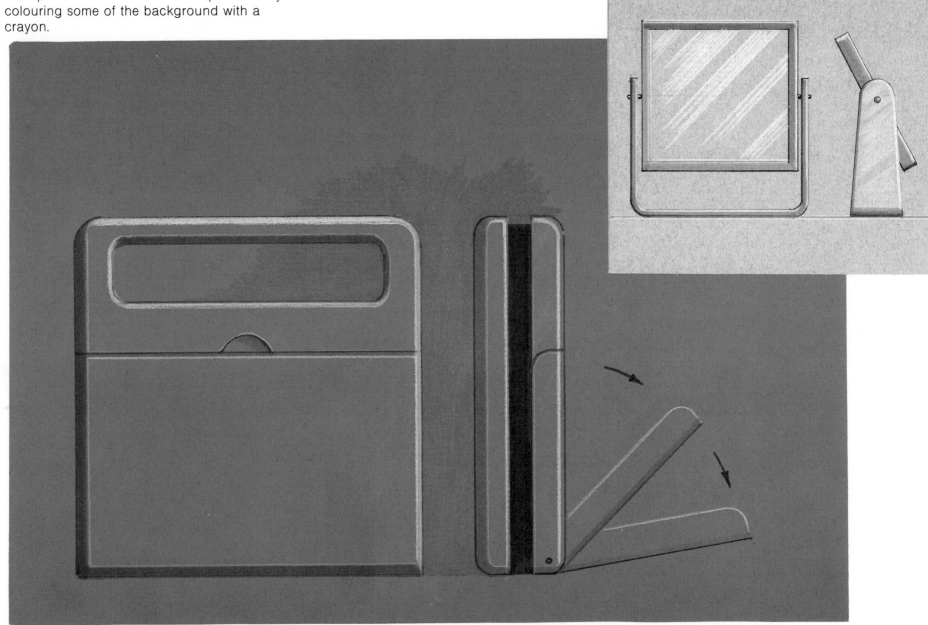

The drawings on this page are all pictorial views of objects drawn on coloured paper. Surfaces as well as edges have been darkened and lightened in order to pick out the form of the object. Can you see that on some of the drawings a shadow has been added? The shadows have been drawn with a colour which is a darker tone than the paper. The shadow emphasises the form of the object and suggests a background.

If you draw with a white crayon or pastel on dark paper, you can produce high contrast highlights and reflections. This effect is useful for illustrating transparent or metallic objects.

Choice of paper

One of the best types of paper to use for this technique is Ingres paper. It can be obtained in a wide range of colours and has a good surface to draw on. However, sugar paper or plain coloured wrapping paper can be used as a less expensive alternative.

Unless the object you are drawing is brightly coloured, it is best to use a background paper of a subdued colour, similar to the ones used on these pages.

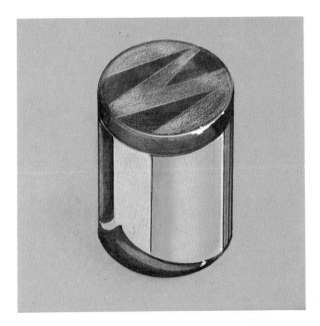

Model Making 1

It is often helpful to make models in the early stages of solving a design problem. Quick and easily made models can act as three-dimensional sketches of design solutions. As a model may be viewed from all sides you will find it easier to judge whether your design looks right, and spot any faults. You will often find that a model will stimulate and promote new ideas, and help you decide on suitable ways of constructing the final design. If the model shows that your design is faulty, you will need to adjust your original idea. It is far better to discover a fault at this stage than later, when much time, effort or money may have been wasted. There are several types of models. You will need to choose the one that is most suitable for your design.

Presentation models

These may be perfect imitations of the final product. They are popular with professional designers when they wish to show clients how a design will look when it has been made.

Soft or sketch models

These are produced early in the design process. They are made from easily worked materials such as card and expanded polystyrene. Sketch models do not usually show detail, but give an impression of the possible design solution.

Small scale models

When designing fairly large items e.g. furniture, it is more convenient to make a model that is smaller than life size. In such areas as interior design, small scale models act as three-dimensional diagrams, and are used to give an idea of room layouts, seating arrangement etc.

Full size models

A model or *mock-up* built full-size can be very valuable for making decisions about dimensions and for testing to see if the design is ergonomically correct.

Large scale models

At times it may be necessary to make a model much larger than the actual design. When designing small items, such as jewellery, or detailed mechanisms, such as a locking device, they will be much easier to study and work on if the scale of the model is enlarged.

Cutaway models

These are models which have had a piece removed in order to expose the inside of the model. They are used to show mechanisms or details of the design construction that cannot be seen from the outside.

Working models

Working models are actually intended to operate. They usually have a mechanism that imitates the final design. This type of model is often used in technology projects to demonstrate how a system or structure behaves, for example a cantilever bridge or traffic light system.

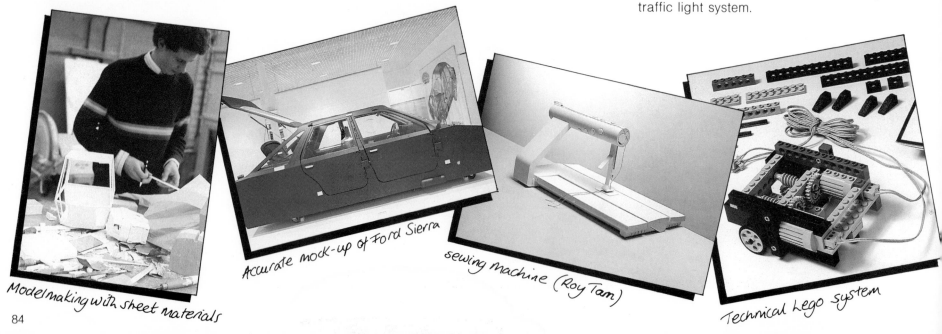

Modelmaking with sheet materials

Accurate mock-up of Ford Sierra

sewing machine (Roy Tam)

Technical Lego system

Suitable model making materials

It is important that you select a material that is suitable for the type of model you wish to make. Easily worked materials like paper and foam are ideal for quick model making. However, they may not be suitable for obtaining the amount of detail that is needed for a presentation model. You should make your model from material that has similar properties to the material you intend to use in the final product. For example, if the design is to be constructed of sheet material, such as acrylic, use sheet material such as card for the model.

Frameworks:

    Art straws — these are larger than drinking straws
    String — may be stiffened with resin or glue
    Wire — soft wires are easier to work with
    Wooden strips — dowelling, balsa strips, narrow off-cuts
    Construction kits — Meccano, Fischer Technic, Lego

Sheet Materials:

    Paper and card — available in a large range of colours and thicknesses.
    Plastic sheet — ABS, sheet polystyrene and rigid PVC can be used for vacuum forming
    Wood — veneers, thin balsa, plywood and hardboard
    Metal — thin sheet and foil

Solid forms:

    Papier maché — good for creating irregular shapes, such as landscapes. Strong when several layers are built up
    Plasticine — easy to sculpt and form. Can be re-used
    Plasticine clay — wax based, used a lot in car styling. Excellent finish is possible
    Clay — can be messy but easy to form, will set hard
    Plaster of Paris — can be cast, quick setting, easy to carve
    Plastic foams — styrofoam, expanded polystyrene. Best cut with hot wire cutter, but beware of fumes. Some foams (such as polyurethane foam — which should not be cut with a hot wire) can be shaped with files and glasspaper
    Woods — jelutong and balsa are light and easy to work with

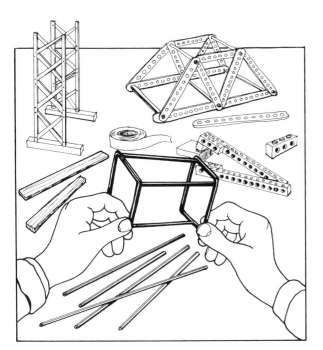

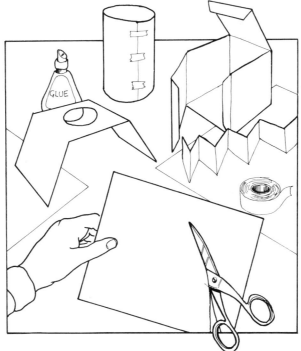

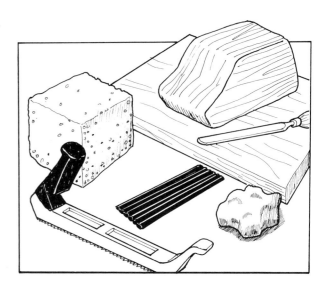

Model Making 3

Kettle Design ①

Styrofoam Models

Kettle Design ②

Vacuum formed Body

③ Kettle Design

④ Kettle Design — Finished Model

Vehicle Design ①

Clay on Wood Base

Vehicle Design ②

Clay Model

Vehicle Design ③

Primer / Filler Basecoat

Vehicle Design ④

Finished Model

Bicycle — Finished Model

Keyboard — Finished Model

Lawn Mower — Finished Model

Car Interior

It is often the techniques used in the final presentation of an idea that give impact to the drawing. For example, a drawing which 'floats' on a blank sheet of paper will not focus or hold our attention. Enclosing your drawing within a frame will attract the eye and help make the drawing 'sit' on the page (figure 87:1).

Figure 87

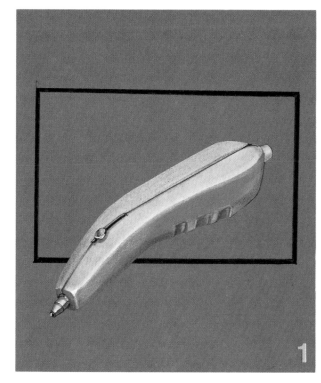

■ Placing a coloured shape behind the object will make it stand out and it will appear more 3-dimensional. The shape can also draw attention to particular details or areas. (Figure 87:2)

■ A background can be used to suggest surroundings, or make the object appear to stand on a surface. This can be done simply by drawing in an horizon line (figure 87:3) or showing the shadows cast by the object.

Lettering 1

How well do you think you could follow a street map with the names of the streets missing from it? In a similar way, design sketches without notes of explanation are often difficult to understand. We can use words to explain those ideas we are unable to draw.

Any lettering that we use, whether for notes, titles or headings must be clear and easy to read. Design drawings can be spoiled by poor lettering. Good use of lettering will not only give information, but can improve the presentation of a drawing.

° HAND LETTERING °

- FOR BEST RESULTS, LETTERING CAN BE CONSTRUCTED BETWEEN TWO HORIZONTAL GUIDELINES (OR USE LINED, OR GRAPH PAPER UNDER-NEATH)
- GUIDELINES SHOULD BE NO WIDER THAN 5mm APART.
- 'LOWER CASE' LETTERS — (a, b, c, d, etc.) CAN BE DRAWN BETWEEN LINES 3mm APART
- POSITION NOTES IN NEAT COLUMNS OR BLOCKS RATHER THAN SCATTERED AT ODD ANGLES OVER THE PAPER. YOU SHOULD BE ABLE TO READ THE NOTES WITHOUT TURNING THE DRAWING SHEET.
- KEEP LETTERS SIMPLE — AVOID FANCY STYLES!

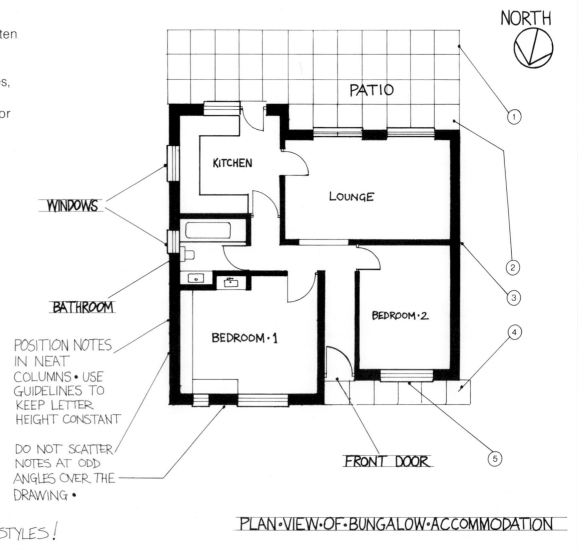

NORTH

PATIO

KITCHEN

LOUNGE

WINDOWS

BATHROOM

BEDROOM·2

BEDROOM·1

POSITION NOTES IN NEAT COLUMNS • USE GUIDELINES TO KEEP LETTER HEIGHT CONSTANT

DO NOT SCATTER NOTES AT ODD ANGLES OVER THE DRAWING •

FRONT DOOR

PLAN·VIEW·OF·BUNGALOW·ACCOMMODATION

YOUR NAME PRINTED NEATLY	TITLE & DETAILS OF DRAWING	SCALE	DATE	DRG.Nº

Dry transfer lettering

Neat, professional looking lettering can be achieved by using *dry transfer letters* As it can be expensive and time-consuming, this type of lettering is best used for headings and titles, where not too many words are needed.

■ Draw a feint pencil line (figure 89:1). This will act as a guide for positioning the letters (figure 89:2).
■ Remove the backing paper from the instant lettering sheet.
■ Rub over the letter on the sheet with a blunt pencil or a burnishing tool. When the letter has turned grey you will know that it has transferred onto the paper (figure 89:3).
■ Remove the instant lettering sheet.
■ If the letter has been transferred to the correct position, it is a good idea to fix it more securely to the page. You can do this by placing the backing sheet over the letter and rubbing it over with a blunt pencil. This is called *burnishing* (figure 89:4).
■ If the letter is *not* in the correct position it can be lifted off the page with sticky tape. This must be done before burnishing.

Stencil lettering

A stencil is a plastic sheet which has letters pierced out of it, (figure 89:5). It acts as a guide for producing neat lettering. Stencils can be obtained with many different styles and sizes of lettering. Some stencils are specially designed for use with a technical pen and ink. As with other forms of lettering, a guideline must be used to help position the letters.

Figure 89

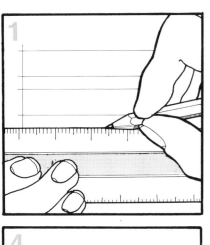

Presentation Drawing 1

A *presentation drawing* should give a clear picture of how a design will look when it is produced. Sometimes this type of drawing is called an artists impression.

A designer will use a presentation drawing to show a client what the finished product will look like. They can discuss the ideas, and final decisions can be made about the design. It·is easier at this stage to make changes to the design than it is after the idea has been put into production. *Figure 90* 1

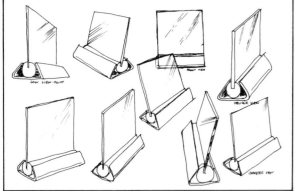

Obviously a presentation drawing must show your design idea off to its best advantage. Begin by selecting the best views of your design (figure 90:1). This should be the view which has the most impact, gives the most information or highlights a particular feature you wish to show.

To make the drawing convincing you will need to give a realistic impression of the finish and the materials that will be used on the actual product. In order to do this you may find it necessary to use different drawing materials together on one illustration. For example, you might use markers together with pastels and pencil crayons. This drawing should stand out from your other drawings as the final solution. Borders, backgrounds and the use of titles and labels with neat lettering will help you achieve this.

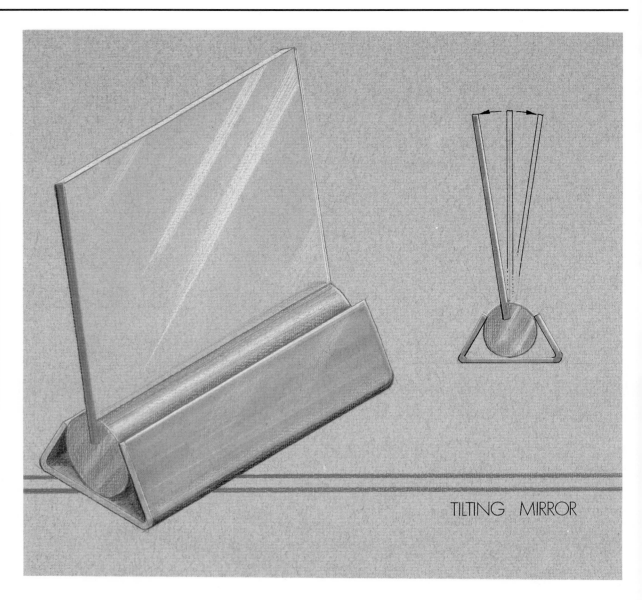

TILTING MIRROR

Mirror tile: pastel rubbed with cotton wool over Ingres paper; highlighted with putty rubber
Round section: blue grey pencil crayon; highlights with white crayon

Acrylic holder: studio marker applied in parallel strokes; highlighted with white crayon darkened on shade areas with pencil crayon
Detail on edges: fine-line marker

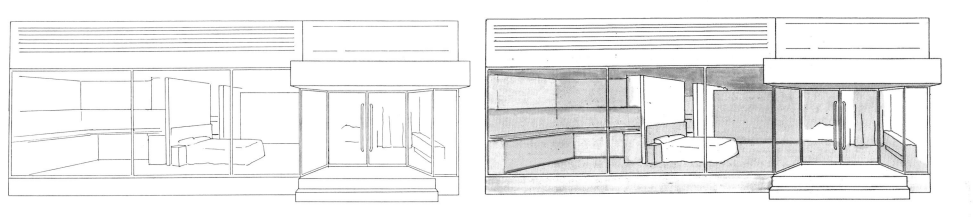

Presentation drawing for a furniture shop front: 1, an outline drawing; 2, colours 'blocked in' with marker pens; 3 details added with fine line marker, air brush and gouache

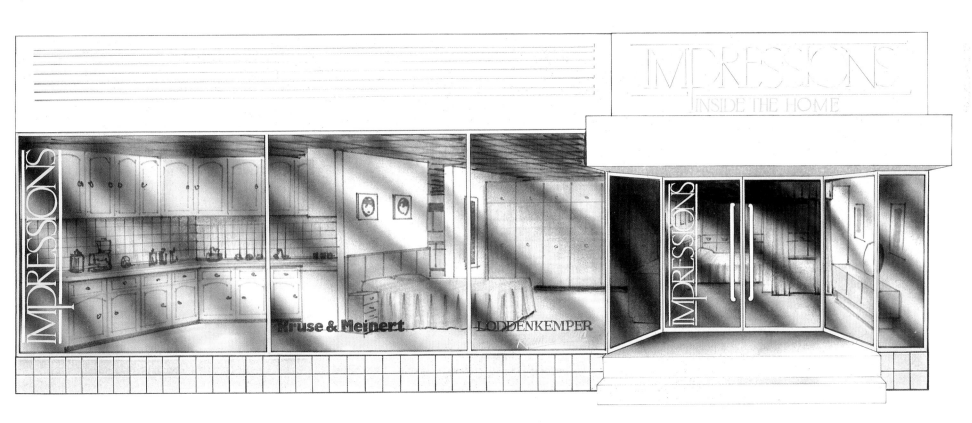

Assignments 6

1 Young children often accidentally lock themselves inside bathrooms. Design and make a working model of a safety lock, that can be opened from the outside. (See pages 84, 85 and 86.)

2 Using modelling as a major part of your presentation, produce design ideas for an emergency shelter. This should be suitable for housing a small group of people made homeless by a disaster such as an earthquake or flood. Your designs must be easy to transport and quick to assemble. (See pages 84, 85 and 86.)

3 Produce design sketches and presentation drawing for one of the following:
(i)   a camera for under 12-year olds,
(ii) a night-light for an infant,
(iii) a young child's calculator.
Take into account the age-group you are designing for, by using appropriate colour schemes or including a novelty feature. You need only be concerned with the appearance of the product not the working parts. (see pages 81–83, 90 and 91)

4 You have been asked to design an eye-catching window display for a large department store. The display is to be animated (have movement) and will contain a mechanism of some sort to achieve this.

You are supplied with one electric motor, and an assortment of gears, pulleys and belts.

(a) Draw diagrams to show how you will achieve movement in the display, and how the parts will be assembled.

(b) Produce a working model. You may wish to use a technical construction kit. Use lightweight modelling material for the display, such as card, balsa, expanded polystyrene or fabric.

5 A museum gift shop is selling a range of printed-card models which may be cut out, folded and glued together. The theme is 'Housing through the ages'. Figure 92:1 shows the front elevations of 3 different houses.

(a) Choose one house and add side and rear views to complete a card development. Chimneys, porches etc. may be added as separate pieces. (See page 15.)

(b) Choose a colour scheme for use on your completed model.

14th century long-house

15th century box-frame farmhouse

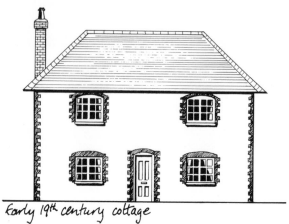

Figure 92 **1**

Early 19th century cottage

Design Project

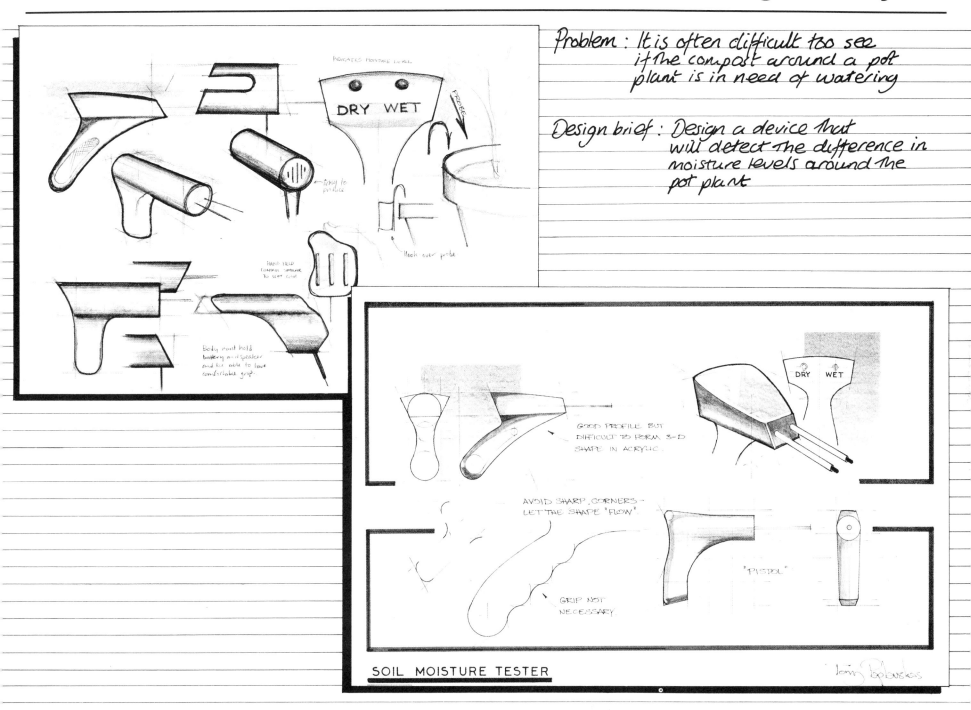

Problem: It is often difficult too see if the compost around a pot plant is in need of watering

Design brief: Design a device that will detect the difference in moisture levels around the pot plant

DRY WET

INDICATES MOISTURE LEVEL

Easy to produce

Hook over probe

HAND HELD CONTROL SIMILAR TO SLOT CAR

Body must hold battery and speaker and be able to have comfortable grip.

GOOD PROFILE BUT DIFFICULT TO FORM 3-D SHAPE IN ACRYLIC.

AVOID SHARP CORNERS - LET THE SHAPE "FLOW".

GRIP NOT NECESSARY

"PISTOL"

SOIL MOISTURE TESTER

Development drawings

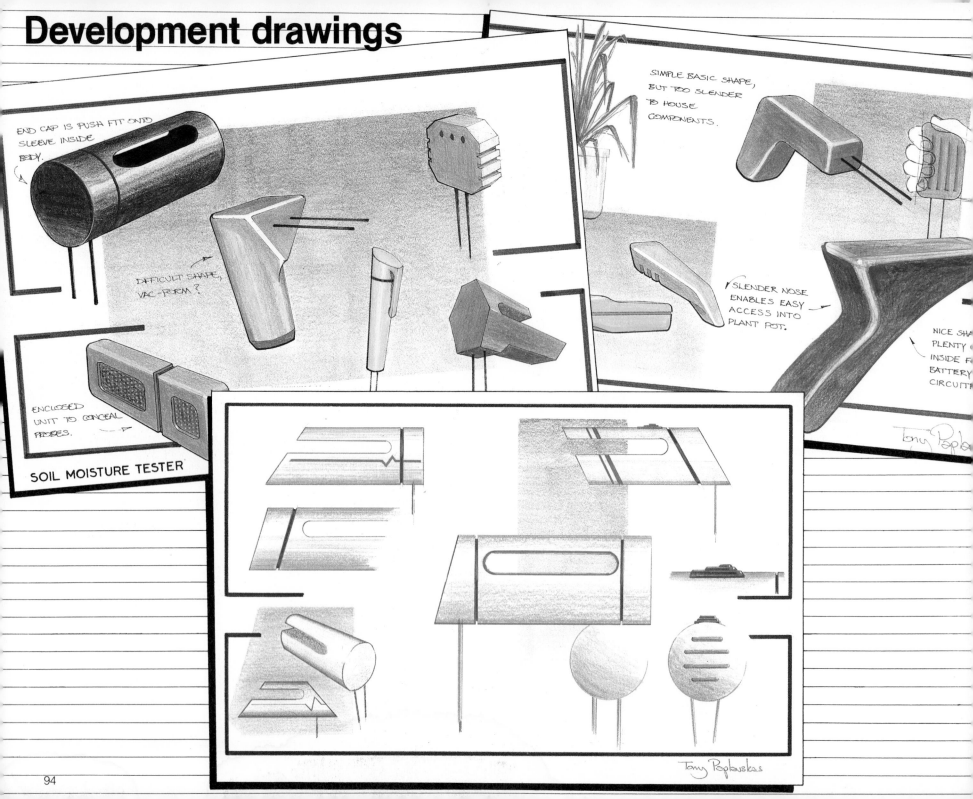

END CAP IS PUSH FIT ONTO SLEEVE INSIDE BODY.

DIFFICULT SHAPE, VAC-FORM ?

ENCLOSED UNIT TO CONCEAL PROBES.

SOIL MOISTURE TESTER

SIMPLE BASIC SHAPE, BUT TOO SLENDER TO HOUSE COMPONENTS.

SLENDER NOSE ENABLES EASY ACCESS INTO PLANT POT.

NICE SHA... PLENTY ... INSIDE F... BATTERY ... CIRCUITT...

Tony Pop...

Tony Poplauskas

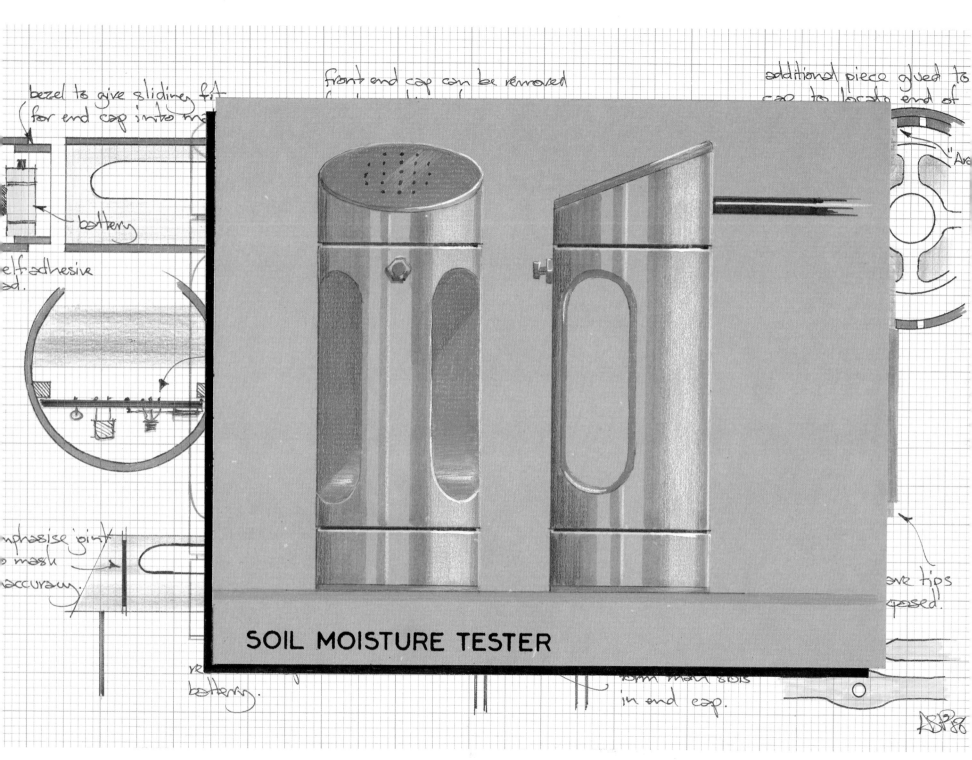

additional piece glued to cap to locate end of

bezel to give sliding fit (for end cap into me...

battery

self-adhesive ad.

emphasise joint to mask accuracy.

battery.

...ve tips ...posed.

...in end cap.

SOIL MOISTURE TESTER

ASP 86

Index